Cⲧⲛ ⲑⲉⲱ Ⲓⲥⲭⲧⲣⲟⲥ

The Feast of the Cross

with an Introduction by His Grace Bishop Serapion

St. Athanasius and St. Cyril Theological Library

Published and Distributed by St. Paul Brotherhood Press

THE FEAST OF THE CROSS

ISBN 978-0-9800065-9-9
LCC in Catalogue Data 2009
Cataloging-in-Publication Data is available on request from the
Library of Congress.

All references from the Old Testament, otherwise noted, are taken from
the English Translation of the Septuagint from the Apostles Bible
copyright © Paul Esposito, with permission. All rights reserved. All
references from the New Testament, unless otherwise noted, are taken
from the New King James Version, copyright © 1982 Thomas Nelson
Publishing, Inc. with permission. All rights reserved.

Coptic Orthodox Diocese of Los Angeles, Southern California, and Hawaii
St. Athanasius and St. Cyril Theological Library
4909 Cleland Avenue, Los Angeles, California 90042

On the Web: www.copticlibrary.org
E-mail: admin@copticlibrary.org

His Holiness Pope Shenouda III

117th Pope and Patriarch of the
Great See of the City of Alexandria

His Grace Bishop Serapion

Bishop of the Coptic Orthodox Diocese of
Los Angeles, Southern California, and Hawaii

TABLE OF CONTENTS

TABLE OF CONTENTS

PREFACE

As a mother feeds her child with the proper food, at the proper time, and using the proper utensils, the Church feeds us the Word of God at different times of the year using the golden spoon of the Fathers. In all wisdom, tender care, and love, our Mother the Church yearns to feed her children the Holy Scriptures and to nourish them with the Bread of Life.

With great joy and enthusiasm, we present to you this book, part of the *Treasures of the Fathers of the Church* series, on the Feasts of the Cross, which are celebrated in the Coptic Orthodox calendar on 17 Tout (September 27 or 28) and 10 Baramhat (March 19).

The Holy Cross held a prominent and revered place in early Christian life and worship. It was a sign of protection, holiness, worship, and blessing to believers everywhere, even before The Empress Helen discovered its location.

In the early third century, for example, Christians made the sign of the Cross on their foreheads three times daily as a sign of protection. In 211, the scholar Tertullian wrote, "At every forward step and movement, at every going in and out, when we put on our clothes and shoes, when we bathe, when we sit at table, when we light the lamps, on couch, on seat, in all the ordinary actions of daily life, we trace upon the forehead the sign [of the Cross]."[1] Another early Christian work of the same period, the *Apostolic Tradition*, reveals the importance of the sign of the Cross in early Christian spirituality and devotion:

> If you are tempted, seal your foreheads reverently. For this is the Sign of the Passion, displayed and made manifest against the devil, provided that you do it with faith, not to be seen by men, but by presenting it with skill like a shield. Because the Adversary, when he sees the strength of the heart and when he sees the inner man which is animated by the Word show, formed on the exterior, the interior image of the Word, he is made to flee by the Spirit

---

[1] Tertullian, *De Corona Militis (On the Military Guard)*, 3; ANF v. 3.

which is in you. This is symbolized by the Paschal lamb which was sacrificed, the blood of which Moses sprinkled on the threshold, and smeared on the doorposts. He told us of the faith which is now in us, which was given to us through the perfect Lamb. By signing [the Cross on] the forehead and eyes with the hand, we turn aside the one who is seeking to destroy us.[2]

By the fourth century, catechumens were instructed that they should make the sign of the Cross to arm themselves against the devil.[3] The sign of the Cross was even used in the earliest rites of baptism in the blessing of the waters, the Chrism, and in the exorcism of catechumens.[4] St. Caesarius of Arles advised his faithful, "Whenever you have to go anywhere, sign yourselves with the Name of Jesus Christ, say the Creed or the Lord's prayer and go your ways sure of the divine protection."[5]

The Cross was not only a sign of protection, but also a sign of worship and veneration, as well. Since at least the second century, early Christians (especially those in Syria) painted or nailed a cross on the eastern wall of a Christian dwelling so that they could face the cross while praying to the East.[6] The martyr Hipparchus worshipped before such a painted cross seven times a day.[7] Christians began their prayers with the sign of the cross, even

[2] *Apostolic Constitutions* 42:1-3.

[3] Nicetas of Remesiana (c. 335-414), the patron saint of Rumania; Jungmann, 20; Fr. J. Dölger, *Sol salutis* (Münster, 2nd ed, 1925), p. 110n;

[4] *Apostolic Tradition*, 20:7 (Chrismation), 21:23; William Harmless, *Augustine and the Catechumenate* (Collegeville, 1995), pp. 274-293 (esp. pages 282, 308, 310, 150).

[5] *S. Caesarii Arelatensis Sermones*, ed. Morin (1937), p. 226; Jungmann, 20.

[6] Joseph A. Jungmann, *Christian Prayer through the* Centuries, (New York: Paulist Press, 2007), p. 8; E. Peterson, *Frühkirche, Judentum und Gnosis*, (Freiburg, 1959), pp. 15-35.

[7] Jungman, 8; Peterson, 9; S. E. Assemani, *Act ass. Martyrium* II (Rome, 1748), p. 125.

during the midnight office.[8] St. Horsiesios (c. 380), the second successor of St. Pachomius, the great Egyptian abbot who established the first rule of monasticism, spoke of the Cross as the heart of monastic piety in Egypt: "We have renounced the word and begun to follow the standard of the Cross."[9] By the seventh century, each Syrian monk had a cross in his cell which he would venerate.[10]

Moreover, the sign of the Cross was a remembrance of the redemption by the Lord's suffering and Crucifixion, which the believers were to commemorate during the third, sixth and ninth hours of the day.[11] The Paradise of the Desert Fathers explains to us how often they would extend their arms in the form of a Cross in prayer, as St. Arsenius did all evening until sunset.[12] In the Divine Liturgy, St. Augustine instructs, "Let them all sign themselves with the sign of the Cross of Christ. Let them all respond, 'Amen.' Let them all sing, 'Alleluia.'"[13] So, the Coptic

---

[8] "Around midnight rise and wash your hands with water and pray...By catching your breath in your hand and signing yourself with the moisture of your breath, your body is purified, even to the feet" (*Apostolic Tradition*, 41:11-13).

[9] St. Horsiesios, *Liber Orsiesii*. Jungmann, 8 (note 43); *Doctrina de inst. Monachorum*, ch. 30 (PG 40, p. 883); H. Bacht, "Studien zum '*Liber Orsiesii*'" *Historisches Jahrbuch* 77 (1958):98-124. A. Veilleux, *Pachomian Koinonia. Vol. 3, Instructions, Letters, and Other Writings of St. Pachomius and His Disciples* (Kalamazoo: Cistercian Studies Series 47,1982); Armand Veilleux, "Horsiesios (St.)," *Coptic Encyclopedia*, vol. 4, edited by Aziz S. Atiya, (New York: Macmillan,1991).

[10] According to the Dadisho the ascetic. See Jungmann, p. 9; Peterson, pp. 17f; Richard Viladesau, *The Beauty of the Cross: The Passion of Christ in Theology and the Arts from the Catecombs to the Eve of the Reformation* (Oxford, 2006), pp. 110-115.

[11] *Apostolic Tradition* 41:5-8, St. Cyprian, *On the Lord's Prayer*, 4:4-35.

[12] *Apophthegmata Patrum*, no. 2.

[13] Harmless, 329.

doxology of the Feast of the Cross begins by saying, "And we also the people, the sons of the Orthodox, we bow down to the Cross, of our Lord Jesus Christ... Hail to you, O Cross, the sign of salvation."

Finally, the Cross for early Christians was a great blessing. The scholar Tertullian understood Jacob's blessing of Ephraim and Mannesseh[14] as a type of the Cross, through which we are blessed.[15] In the fourth century, the pilgrim Egeria describes how people would take the blessing of the bishop by kissing the cross in his hands. Above all, the feasts of the Cross remind us of this great blessing of the Cross, especially in its hymns and praises. As the festal doxology declares:

> We take pride in you, O Cross; on which Jesus was crucified, for through your type, we were set free. The mouths of the Orthodox, and the seven angelic hosts, take pride in you, O Cross, of our Good Savior. We carry you O Cross, on the necks of the Christians, O supporter of the brave, and we proclaim loudly: "Hail to you, O Cross, the joy of Christians, the conquer of tyranny, our confirmation we the faithful. Hail to you, O Cross, the comfort of the faithful, and the confirmation of the martyrs, who completed their struggles."

This volume consists of eight chapters. After presenting the readings for these feasts, the next chapter contains a thorough introduction to the Feast by our beloved father, His Holiness Pope Shenouda III. May our Good Lord keep him for us for many years and peaceful times to shepherd the Church of God with wisdom, might, and every spiritual virtue. The following chapters include various excerpts from historical accounts of the finding of the Cross, as well as theological and biblical meditations on the Cross

---

[14] See Gen. 48.

[15] "But this also comes of an ancient mystery wherein Jacob blessed his grandsons born of Joseph, Ephraim and Manasseh, his hands being laid upon their heads, and interchanged, and turned indeed crosswise, the one over the other, so that, representing Christ in a figure, they might even then foreshow the blessing to be accomplished in Christ." (*De Baptismo* 8.8)

by the Fathers of the Church, with a special segment by one of the Catechetical Homilies attributed to St. Cyril of Jerusalem.

As with all of the books in the *Treasures of the Fathers of the Church* series, the paramount objective of this work is to introduce the believers to the "trialogue" of faith – the harmony among the Holy Scriptures, the Church Fathers and the Church. Through this symphony of discourse, the believer not only reads the Holy Scriptures, but understands it through the homilies and commentaries of the Fathers of the Church, as well as through the Church life itself. This is a "companion" to the Coptic Orthodox Lectionary.

We hope and pray that this work not only introduces each believer to the Holy Scriptures, the Church Fathers and the Church rites, but also provides a deep source of blessing, wisdom and faith. Just as the Lord of Hosts promised to Baruch the prophet, "But I will give you life, as finding a treasure in every place, wherever you go" (Jeremiah 51:35), we experience that in every place we search in the Scriptures with the fathers lies a discovery of precious treasure for our souls – truly, the Pearl of great price, our Lord Jesus Christ.

May the blessing of the power of the live-giving Cross be with us, keep us from every evil all the days of our life, through the never-ending intercessions of the Holy Theotokos St. Mary, and the prayers of all His angels, St. Paul the Apostle, and the rest of the apostles, martyrs, and saints who have pleased Him since the beginning, we pray that this work will be a source of blessing for the glory of His Name and the spreading of His Kingdom.

Glory be to the Holy Trinity, our God, unto the ages of all ages, Amen.

Bishop Serapion
Feast of the Cross 2009

§ ✞ ɛ

SCRIPTURAL READINGS FOR THE FEASTS OF THE HOLY CROSS

EVENING RAISING OF INCENSE

From the Psalms of David the Prophet and King. May his blessing be with us, Amen.

There are many who say, "Who will show us any good?" LORD, lift up the light of Your countenance upon us. You have put gladness in my heart, More than in the season that their grain and wine increased. I will both lie down in peace, and sleep; For You alone, O LORD, make me dwell in safety (Psalms 4:6-8).

A reading from the Holy Gospel according to St. John the Apostle and Evangelist. May his blessing be with us, Amen.

Then Jesus said to them, "When you lift up the Son of Man, then you will know that I am He, and that I do nothing of Myself; but as My Father taught Me, I speak these things. And He who sent Me is with Me. The Father has not left Me alone, for I always do those things that please Him." As He spoke these words, many believed in Him. Then Jesus said to those Jews who believed Him, "If you abide in My word, you are My disciples indeed. And you shall know the truth, and the truth shall make you free." They answered Him, "We are Abraham's descendants, and have never been in bondage to anyone. How can You say, 'You will be made free'?" Jesus answered them, "Most assuredly, I say to you, whoever commits sin is a slave of sin. And a slave does not abide in the house forever, but a son abides forever. Therefore if the Son makes you free, you shall be free indeed. "I know that you are Abraham's descendants, but you seek to kill Me, because My word has no place in you. I speak what I have seen with My Father, and you do what you have seen with your father." They answered and said to Him, "Abraham is our father." Jesus said to them, "If you were Abraham's children, you would do the works of Abraham. But now you seek to kill Me, a Man who has told you the truth which I heard from God. Abraham did not do this. You do the deeds of your father." Then they said to Him, "We were not born of fornication; we have one Father—God." Jesus said to them, "If God were your Father, you would love Me, for I proceeded forth and came from God; nor have I come of Myself, but He sent Me" (John 8:28-42).

MORNING RAISING OF INCENSE

From the Psalms of David the Prophet and King. May his blessing be with us, Amen.

You have given a banner to those who fear You, That it may be displayed because of the truth. That Your beloved may be delivered, Save with Your right hand, and hear me (Psalms 60:4-5).

A reading from the Holy Gospel according to St. John the Apostle and Evangelist. May his blessing be with us, Amen.

"If anyone serves Me, let him follow Me; and where I am, there My servant will be also. If anyone serves Me, him My Father will honor. Now My soul is troubled, and what shall I say? 'Father, save Me from this hour'? But for this purpose I came to this hour. Father, glorify Your name." Then a voice came from heaven, saying, "I have both glorified it and will glorify it again." Therefore the people who stood by and heard it said that it had thundered. Others said, "An angel has spoken to Him." Jesus answered and said, "This voice did not come because of Me, but for your sake. Now is the judgment of this world; now the ruler of this world will be cast out. And I, if I am lifted up from the earth, will draw all peoples to Myself." This He said, signifying by what death He would die. The people answered Him, "We have heard from the law that the Christ remains forever; and how can You say, 'The Son of Man must be lifted up'? Who is this Son of Man?" Then Jesus said to them, "A little while longer the light is with you. Walk while you have the light, lest darkness overtake you; he who walks in darkness does not know where he is going. While you have the light, believe in the light, that you may become sons of light."

These things Jesus spoke, and departed, and was hidden from them (John 12:26-36).

DIVINE LITURGY

Paul, the servant of the Lord, called to be an apostle and appointed to the gospel of God. A reading from the First Epistle of St. Paul to the Corinthians. May his blessing be with us, Amen.

For Christ did not send me to baptize, but to preach the gospel, not with wisdom of words, lest the Cross of Christ should be made of no effect. For the message of the Cross is foolishness to those who are perishing, but to us who are being saved it is the power of God. For it is written: "I will destroy the wisdom of the wise, And bring to nothing the understanding of the prudent." Where is the wise? Where is the scribe? Where is the disputer of this age? Has not God made foolish the wisdom of this world? For since, in the wisdom of God, the world through wisdom did not know God, it pleased God through the foolishness of the message preached to save those who believe. For Jews request a sign, and Greeks seek after wisdom; but we preach Christ crucified, to the Jews a stumbling block and to the Greeks foolishness, but to those who are called, both Jews and Greeks, Christ the power of God and the wisdom of God. Because the foolishness of God is wiser than men, and the weakness of God is stronger than men. For you see your calling, brethren, that not many wise according to the flesh, not many mighty, not many noble, are called. But God has chosen the foolish things of the world to put to shame the wise, and God has chosen the weak things of the world to put to shame the things which are mighty; and the base things of the world and the things which are despised God has chosen, and the things which are not, to bring to nothing the things that are, that no flesh should glory in His presence. But of Him you are in Christ Jesus, Who became for us Wisdom from God—and righteousness and sanctification and redemption– that, as it is written, "He who glories, let him glory in the LORD" (1 Corinthians 1:17-31).

The Catholic Epistle of our Teacher, St. Peter the Apostle may His blessings be with us all. My beloved...

Beloved, I beg you as sojourners and pilgrims, abstain from fleshly lusts which war against the soul, having your conduct honorable among the Gentiles, that when they speak against you as evildoers, they may, by your good works which they observe, glorify God in the day of visitation. Therefore submit yourselves to every ordinance of man for the Lord's sake, whether to the king as supreme, or to governors, as to those who are sent by him for the punishment of evildoers and for the praise of those who do good. For this is the will of God, that by doing good you may put to silence the ignorance of foolish men–as free, yet not using liberty as a cloak for vice, but as bondservants of God. Honor all people. Love the brotherhood. Fear God. Honor the king. Servants, be submissive to your masters with all fear, not only to the good and gentle, but also to the harsh. For this is commendable, if because of conscience toward God one endures grief, suffering wrongfully. For what credit is it if, when you are beaten for your faults, you take it patiently? But when you do good and suffer, if you take it patiently, this is commendable before God. For to this you were called, because Christ also suffered for us, leaving us an example, that you should follow His steps: "Who committed no sin, nor was deceit found in His mouth"; who, when He was reviled, did not revile in return; when He suffered, He did not threaten, but committed Himself to Him Who judges righteously; Who Himself bore our sins in His own Body on the tree, that we, having died to sins, might live for righteousness–by Whose stripes you were healed. For you were like sheep going astray, but have now returned to the Shepherd and Overseer of your souls (1 Peter 2:11-25).

The Acts of our fathers the Apostles. May their blessings be with us, Amen.

Then Peter opened his mouth and said: "In truth I perceive that God shows no partiality. But in every nation whoever fears Him and works righteousness is accepted by Him. The word which God sent to the children of Israel, preaching peace through Jesus Christ–He is Lord of all–that word you know, which was proclaimed throughout all Judea, and began from Galilee after the baptism which John preached: how God anointed Jesus of Nazareth with the Holy Spirit and with power, Who went about doing good and healing all who were oppressed by the devil, for God was with Him. And we are witnesses of all things which He did both in the land of the Jews and in Jerusalem, Whom they killed by hanging on a tree. Him God raised up on the third day, and showed Him openly, not to all the people, but to witnesses chosen before by God, even to us who ate and drank with Him after He arose from the dead. And He commanded us to preach to the people, and to testify that it is He who was ordained by God to be Judge of the living and the dead. To Him all the prophets witness that, through His name, whoever believes in Him will receive remission of sins" (Acts 10:34-43).

From the Psalms of David the Prophet and King. May his blessing be with us, Amen.

"Praise is awaiting You, O God, in Zion; And to You the vow shall be performed. O You who hear prayer, To You all flesh will come" (Psalms 65:1-2).

A reading from the Holy Gospel according to St. John the Apostle and Evangelist. May his blessing be with us, Amen.

Now it was the Feast of Dedication in Jerusalem, and it was winter. And Jesus walked in the temple, in Solomon's porch. Then the Jews surrounded Him and said to Him, "How long do You keep us in doubt? If You are the Christ, tell us plainly." Jesus answered them, "I told you, and you do not believe. The works that

I do in My Father's Name, they bear witness of Me. But you do not believe, because you are not of My sheep, as I said to you. My sheep hear My voice, and I know them, and they follow Me. And I give them eternal life, and they shall never perish; neither shall anyone snatch them out of My hand. My Father, who has given them to Me, is greater than all; and no one is able to snatch them out of My Father's hand. I and My Father are One." Then the Jews took up stones again to stone Him. Jesus answered them, "Many good works I have shown you from My Father. For which of those works do you stone Me?" The Jews answered Him, saying, "For a good work we do not stone You, but for blasphemy, and because You, being a Man, make Yourself God." Jesus answered them, "Is it not written in your law, 'I said, "You are gods"'? If He called them gods, to whom the Word of God came (and the Scripture cannot be broken), do you say of Him Whom the Father sanctified and sent into the world, "You are blaspheming," because I said, 'I am the Son of God'? If I do not do the works of My Father, do not believe Me; but if I do, though you do not believe Me, believe the works, that you may know and believe that the Father is in Me, and I in Him." (John 10:22-38)

℅ ✚ ℅

THE FEAST OF THE CROSS

His Holiness Pope Shenouda III[1]

---

[1] Edited from the 2nd Edition, September 1999 (Anba Rewis Printing)

T he Church celebrates the Feast of the Cross on 17 Tout (September 27 or 28), the day of the apparition of the Cross to the Emperor Constantine, and on 10 Baramhat (March 19), the day when the Empress Helen found the wood of the Holy Cross.

The Lord Christ and the Cross

The Lord invited us to bear the Cross and said: "If anyone desires to come after Me, let him deny himself, and take up his cross, and follow Me" (Matthew 16:24; Mark 8:34).

And He said to the rich young man: "Go your way, sell whatever you have and give to the poor...and come, take up the Cross, and follow Me" (Mark 10:21).

He made the bearing of the Cross a condition for the discipleship to Him. He said: "And whoever does not bear his cross and come after Me cannot be My disciple" (Luke 14:27).

He, Himself, during all the period of His Incarnation on earth, lived bearing the Cross. Since His nativity, Herod wanted to kill Him, and He fled with His mother to Egypt.

When He began His mission, He suffered the fatigue of service, and had "nowhere to lay His head" (Luke 9:58).

He lived a life of pain, so that Isaiah said about Him that He is: "A Man of sorrow and acquainted with grief" (Isaiah 53:3).

He was bitterly persecuted by the Jews. Once they "took up stones again to stone Him" (John 10:31). Another time they wanted to "throw Him down over the cliff" (Luke 4:29). As for their insults and their accusations of Him, they are very numerous. These are all crosses that are different than the actual Cross on which our Lord was crucified.

The Cross in the Lives of the Saints

The disciples of Christ also placed the Cross before their eyes. They preached it continually saying, "But we preach Christ crucified," although He is "to the Jews a stumbling block and to the Greeks foolishness" (1 Corinthians 1:23).

St. Paul the Apostle said, "For I determined not to know anything among you except Jesus Christ and Him crucified" (1 Corinthians 2:2). He would rather boast in the Cross saying, "But God forbid that I should boast except in the Cross of our Lord Jesus Christ, by whom the world has been crucified to me, and I to the world" (Galatians 6:14).

Even the angel who announced the Resurrection, used this expression "Jesus who was crucified" when He said to the two Mary's "I know that you seek Jesus Who was crucified. He is not here; for He is risen, as He said" (Matthew 28:5). Thus, the evangelist called Him "Jesus Who was crucified" although He was already risen. The expression "Who was crucified" remained attached to Him, and our fathers the apostles used it and concentrated their predication on it. As St. Peter said to the Jews "know assuredly that God has made this Jesus, Whom you crucified, both Lord and Christ" (Acts 2:36).

The Cross is the narrow gate through which the Lord invited us to enter. (Matthew 7:13). He said to us:

✜ "In the world you will have tribulations" (John 16:33).

✜ "And you will be hated by all for My Name's sake" (Matthew 10:22).

✜ "Yes, the time is coming that whoever kills you will think that he offers God service" (John 16:2).

✜ "If you were of the world, the world would love its own. Yet because you are not of the world, but I chose you out of the world, therefore the world hates you" (John 15:19).

✜ Thus the apostle St. Paul taught: "We must through many tribulations enter the kingdom of God" (Acts 14:22).

The life of the Cross is evident in the lives of the martyrs, the patriarchs, and the ascetics. In view of the faith, the martyrs and the confessors suffered unbearable torments and agonies. The majority of the early apostles and bishops marched in the way of martyrdom.

When the Lord called Saul of Tarsus to become an apostle for the Gentiles, He said about him "For I will show him how many things he must suffer for My Name's sake" (Acts 9:16).

We can mention as an example, St. Athanasius the Apostolic of the patriarchs and the cross which they carried. He was exiled three times and he was exposed to false accusations. St. John Chrysostom was also exiled, and the fathers were exposed to much imprisonment and exile.

As for our fathers, the monks, the Church calls them "Cross-bearers" because they have borne the cross of solitude and aloofness from every human consolation, and the cross of asceticism by which they were stripped from every corporal desire. They suffered the pains of hunger, thirst, cold, heat, poverty, and destitution—all because of their great love for Christ, the King. They also suffered the afflictions and the warfare of the devils in various ways and kinds, as in the life of St. Antony, and the lives of the wandering anchorites.

The Cross Precedes Resurrection

Christ was elevated over the level of the earth in His Crucifixion. He was also elevated over the level of the tomb in His Resurrection. He was elevated over the level of all the world in His Ascension to heaven and in His sitting at the right side of the Father. He was rather elevated over the level of this heaven.

These are degrees of elevation, all of which He had begun by the Cross. Before that, He was elevated over the level of self preoccupation in His Nativity. He "made Himself of no reputation, taking the form of a servant" (Philippians 2:7).

The Cross of the Lord preceded His Resurrection; and His making Himself of no reputation preceded His glory. Pain always precedes the crowns. Thus, St. Paul the Apostle said: "if indeed we suffer with Him, that we may also be glorified together" (Romans 8:17). In this way, he showed us the value and the results of pain. He rather considered pain as a gift in life to us from God. He said,

"For to you it has been granted on behalf of Christ, not only to believe in Him, but also to suffer for His sake" (Philippians 1:29).

Pain is considered to be a gift because of its crowns. Our Lord established the bearing of the Cross as a condition to discipleship to Him. He said: "If anyone desires to come after Me, let him deny himself, and take up his cross, and follow Me" (Matthew 16:24). Moreover, He said, "And whoever does not bear his cross and come after Me cannot be My disciple" (Luke 14:27).

Such as the bearing of the Cross is a condition for life with God, so also it is a test of seriousness and steadfastness in His way. The tribulations to which the faithful man is exposed during his life, are a test of the extent of his steadfastness in faith. Thus the Lord said: "in the world you will have tribulation" (John 16:33).

While He was on His way to the Cross, He permitted that His disciples should encounter the bearing of the Cross, so that the extent of their steadfastness should appear. He said, "Satan has asked for you, that he may sift you as wheat" (Luke 22:31).

For this reason, the Holy Church has placed the martyrs in the highest order of saints because they were those who have suffered the Cross more than all the others, in view of their constancy in the faith. The Church places also with them the confessors who confessed the faith and suffered many torments, although they did not obtain the crown of martyrdom.

If you bear a cross, accept it joyfully because of the crowns which you will obtain, if you do not complain and do not doubt.

It was said about the sufferings of Christ our Lord that He, "for the joy that was set before Him, endured the Cross, despising the shame, and has sat down at the right hand of the throne of God" (Hebrews 12:2). Here, we find the Cross with joy in enduring it, and glory resulting from it.

You will encounter many kinds of crosses. Among them, there are exertion, tolerance, patience, fatigue in service, fatigue in repentance, and discipline from God and the fathers.

Do not grumble then, whenever you bear a cross; and do not think that spiritual life must be easy, and its way covered with flowers. Otherwise, on what account will you be rewarded in eternity? Moreover, what is the meaning of the words of the Lord concerning the narrow gate (Matthew 7:13)?

The Christian Life is a Cross

In fact, Christian life is practically a journey to Golgotha; and Christianity without a Cross is really not Christianity.

Those who have received their good things on earth, will have no share in the Kingdom, as the story of the rich man and Lazarus explains to us (Luke 16:25). We say that, regarding individuals, just as we say it regarding groups and churches also.

For Christianity is a participation in the sufferings of Christ, as the apostle St. Paul said: "that I may know Him and the power of His resurrection, and the fellowship of His sufferings, being conformed to His death" (Philippians 3:10). He said also about this participation in the sufferings: "I have been crucified with Christ, it is no longer I who live, but Christ lives in me" (Galatians 2:20).

Therefore if you want to live with Christ, you must be crucified with Christ, or you must be crucified for Him, and suffer for Him, even if that would lead to death for Him also.

The Cross and its Glories

In Christianity, you suffer, you find pleasure in suffering, and you obtain crowns for your suffering which is transformed into glory. Christianity is not a Cross which you carry, and grumble and protest in your complaint! No, but it is the love of the Cross, the love of suffering and sacrifice and fatigue for the Lord and for the expansion of His kingdom.

It was said about the Lord Christ: "Who for the joy that was set before Him endured the Cross, despising the shame" (Hebrews 12:2). The apostle St. Paul said: "Therefore I take pleasure in infirmities, in reproaches, in needs, in persecutions, in distresses, for Christ's sake" (2 Corinthians 12:10). And after having been scourged, the apostles "departed from the presence of the council, rejoicing that they were counted worthy to suffer shame for His name" (Acts 5:41).

But, concerning the glories of sufferings, the apostle says: "If indeed we suffer with Him, that we may also be glorified together" (Romans 8:17). Afterwards, he said: "For I consider that the sufferings of this present time are not worthy to be compared with the glory which shall be revealed in us" (Romans 8:18). And thus, St. Peter the Apostle said, "But even if you should suffer for righteousness' sake, you are blessed" (1 Peter 3:14).

Hence sufferings are accompanied by blessings. The Lord Christ mentioned them saying: "Blessed are you when they revile and persecute you, and say all kinds of evil against you falsely for My sake. Rejoice and be exceedingly glad, for great is your reward in heaven, for so they persecuted the prophets who were before you" (Matthew 5:11-12).

Here we find that the sufferings for the Lord are associated with joy and jubilation and with the celestial reward because after the Cross, there is the Resurrection, the Ascension, and the sitting at the right hand of the Father. If Christianity were only a cross, without glories, people would have been tired, and as the apostle said: "If in this life only we have hope in Christ, we are of all men the most pitiable" (1 Corinthians 15:19). But Christians in their bearing of the Cross, look at the eternal glories "while we do not look at the things which are seen, but at the things which are not seen. For the things which are seen are temporary, but the things which are not seen are eternal" (2 Corinthians 4:18).

Therefore, with external fatigue, there is peace and consolation. While they were stoning him, St. Stephen saw the heavens opened "and saw the glory of God" (Acts 7:55, 56). What joy he had then!

There is another joy which the martyrs felt; it is that they had completed the days of their expatriation on earth and the moment of their encounter with the Lord approached. Some of them saw the crowns and the glories; and some others had holy visions that consoled them.

We do not separate the Cross from its rejoicing and its glories: also we do not separate it from the assistance and grace of God.

The Christian might carry a Cross, but he does not carry it alone, and God does not leave him alone. There is a divine assistance that supports and upholds. It is that assistance which stood with the martyrs till they supported the sufferings, and which stands with the faithful in every tribulation. There is the encouraging expression of the Lord:

- ✟ "Do not be afraid...for I am with you, and no one will attack you to hurt you" (Acts 18: 9,10).

- ✟ "Be strong and of good courage; do not be afraid, nor be dismayed, for the Lord your God is with you wherever you go" (Joshua 1:9).

- ✟ "They will fight against you, but they shall not prevail against you. For I am with you...to deliver you" (Jeremiah 1:19).

The Love of Christianity for the Cross

The Cross is an emblem to which every Christian clings because of its spiritual and doctrinal meanings. We suspend it on the churches, we include it in all our sculptures, we suspend it around our necks, we make its sign on ourselves, we begin our prayers with it, we sign it on our food, we sanctify with it all that we possess. The men of the clergy carry it in their hands, and they bless the people with it.

The Cross is used in all the mysteries of the Church, and in all the signings and the consecrations, in the belief that all the blessings of the New Testament came as a result of the Cross. The clothes of the clerical men are adorned with the Cross, not just for ornamentation, but for its benediction and its power. We celebrate two feasts for the Cross, and we carry the Cross during the processions and the celebrations.

We see that there is a power in the signing of the Cross, which the demons dread. All the pains of the devil to ruin human beings has been lost by means of the deliverance which was realized on the Cross. Therefore Satan dreads the sign of the Cross, on the condition that the signing of the Cross is done with faith and reverence. St. Paul said: "For the message of the Cross is foolishness to those who are perishing, but to us who are being saved it is the power of God" (1 Corinthians 1:18). That is why a Christian fortifies himself with the signing of the Cross.

How to Bear Your Cross Practically

1. The Cross is a sign of love, bestowal, sacrifice, and redemption, which you carry each time you are tired in view of the practice of these virtues.

Tire yourself for the rest of another and for his deliverance and service, and be confident that God never forgets the fatigue of charity: "And each one will receive his own reward according to his own labor" (1 Corinthians 3:8). Train yourself to give: whatever you bestow and support and sacrifice. Train yourself to give from your necessities, as the blessed widow had done (Luke 21:4). Tire yourself in your service, because the more you tire, the more your love will appear, and therefore the greater your sacrifice will be.

2. The Cross is also a sign of suffering and endurance.

In the midst of the sufferings which the Lord endured for us—whether the sufferings of the body, of which He said: "They pierced My hands and My feet; I can count all My bones" (Psalms 21:16-17), or the sufferings of shame which He joyfully endured for us—He was rejoicing for our salvation. Therefore, the apostle said about Him: "Who for the joy that was set before Him endured the Cross, despising the shame" (Hebrews 12:2). How great is the endurance when it is joyfully done. That is a lesson for us.

If you endure the tribulation of a cross for the Lord; if you encounter persecution because of your justness; if you are afflicted by a disease or physical witness as a result; or if you endure the wearisome deeds of people without exacting revenge for yourself, turning the other cheek and walking the second mile, not resisting the evil person (Matthew 5:39), then respond with patience. This is the patience of the Cross and it can manifest itself in your family life, service, or career.

3. You will bear a cross if you crucify the flesh with its passions (cf. Galatians 5:24).

Each time you attempt to overcome a craving or a guilty desire, you are bearing a cross. You also crucify your thoughts each time you control them from wandering. Likewise, when you restrain your senses, bridle your tongue, constrain your body, endure hunger, avoid appetizing food, escape bodily pleasure, and control the love of money, you bear a cross.

4. You bear your cross in self-denial, by taking the last place.

By not seeking dignity, by your giving up your rights, by not taking your reward on earth, by preferring others to yourself in everything with love that "does not seek its own" (1 Corinthians 13:5), by humility and renouncement, and by keeping away from praise and honor.

5. You bear your cross by bearing the sins of others, as our Lord the Christ did.

There is no objection that you would bear the guilt of another one and be punished instead of him; or that you bear the responsibilities of another one, and to carry them on instead of him. As St. Paul said to Philemon about Onesimus: "But if he has wronged you or owes anything, put that on my account. I, Paul, am writing with my own hand. I will repay" (Philemon 18-19).

As much as you can, participate in the sufferings of others, and carry them in their place. Be a Cyrenian bearing the cross of another.

Spiritual Meanings of the Cross

When we make the sign of the Cross, we remember many of the theological and spiritual meanings which are connected to it:

1. We remember the love of God for us, Who accepted death instead of us, in view of our salvation.

"All we like sheep have gone astray, we have turned, every one, to his own way; and the Lord has laid on Him the iniquity of us all" (Isaiah 53:6). When we make the sign of the Cross, we remember "the Lamb of God Who takes away the sin of the world" (John 1:29). "And He Himself is the expitiation for our sins, and not for ours only but also for the whole world" (1 John 2:2).

2. In the Cross, we remember our sins.

Our sins which He has borne on the Cross, and for which He Incarnated and was crucified…With this remembrance, we are humbled, our souls become contrite, and we thank Him for the price which He paid for us "For you were bought at a price; therefore glorify God in your body and in your spirit, which are God's" (1 Corinthians 6:20).

3. In the Cross, we remember the divine justice.

We remember that forgiveness was not because of justice, but the divine justice took what was due on the Cross. We do not then consider sin as a slight matter, the sin whose price is such as that.

4. In our signing of the Cross, we declare our discipleship to this Crucified One.

Those who take the Cross simply by its spiritual meaning, inside the heart, without any apparent sign, do not openly manifest this discipleship. We declare this discipleship in many forms: by doing the sign of the Cross, by carrying the Cross on our breasts, by kissing the Cross in front of everybody, by imprinting it on our wrists, and by raising it above the places in which we worship.

With all this, we openly declare our faith, for we are not ashamed of the Cross of Christ in front of others. Rather, we boast of it, we hold fast to it, we celebrate feasts for it. Even without speaking, our plain aspect manifests our faith.

5. We do not make the sign of the Cross on ourselves in a silent manner, but we concurrently say: "In the Name of the Father, the Son, and the Holy Spirit."

Thus, each time we make the sign of the Cross, we declare our faith in the Holy Trinity Who is One God forever and ever, Amen. The Holy Trinity is continually in our thoughts, and that is not available to those who do not make the sign of the Cross as we do.

6. In making the sign of the Cross, we also declare our belief in Incarnation and Redemption.

When we make the sign of the Cross from upward to downward, and from the left side to the right side, we remember that God has come down from heaven downward to our earth, and transported people from the left side to the right side, from obscurity to light, and from death to life. How many are the meditations which come to our hearts and minds from the signing of the Cross?!

7. We remember the forgiveness in the Cross.

When we look to the Cross, we remember how our sins were forgiven and how our Lord addressed the heavenly Father saying (while He was on the Cross): "Father, forgive them, for they do not know what they do" (Luke 23:34).

8. In the signing of the Cross, there is a religious instruction for our children and for others:

Whoever makes the sign of the Cross, when he prays, when he enters the church, when he eats, when he sleeps, and at every moment, remembers the Cross. This remembrance is spiritually useful and biblically desirable. In it, there is also an instruction for people, that Christ was crucified. This instruction is especially important for our small children, who grow from their childhood being accustomed to the Cross.

9. By making the sign of the Cross, we preach the death of the Lord for us, conforming to His commandment.

Our Lord Who redeemed us commanded us to preach His "death till He comes" (1 Corinthians 11:26). In making the sign of the Cross, we remember His death always, and we keep remembering Him until His Second Coming. We also remember Him in the Mystery of Eucharist. Although this Mystery is not done every moment, we can still make the sign of the Cross at every moment, remembering the death of Christ for our sake.

10. In making the sign of the Cross, we remember that the retribution of sin is death.

Because otherwise Christ would not have died; "we were dead in trespasses" (Ephesians 2:5). Christ died instead of us upon the Cross and gave us life. Having paid the price on the Cross, He said to the Father: "Father, forgive them" (Luke 23:34).

11. In making the sign of the Cross, we remember the love of God for us.

We remember that the Cross is a sacrifice of love. "For God so loved the world that He gave His only begotten Son, that whoever believes in Him should not perish but have everlasting life" (John 3:16).

We also remember that "God demonstrated His own love toward us, in that while we were still sinners, Christ died for us, and we were reconciled to God through the death of His Son" (Romans 5: 8,10).

In the Cross, we remember the love of God for us, because "Greater love has no one than this, than to lay down one's life for his friends" (John 15:13).

12. We make the sign of the Cross because it gives us power.

The apostle St. Paul felt that power of the Cross, and said: "by whom the world has been crucified to me, and I to the world" (Galatians 6:14). He also said: "For the Word of the Cross is foolishness to those who are perishing, but to us who are being saved it is the power of God" (1 Corinthians 1:18).

Note that he did not say that the Crucifixion is the power of God, but he said that the simple word of the Cross is the power of

God. Therefore, when we make the sign of the Cross and when we mention the Cross, we are filled with power; because we remember that the Lord trampled death by the Cross, and He granted life to everybody, and forced and defeated Satan.

Therefore, we make the sign of the Cross, because Satan dreads it: All the labor of Satan since he fought Adam until the end of time, has been lost on the Cross. The Lord has paid the price and erased all the sins of people with His blood, for those who believe and obey. Therefore, whenever Satan sees the Cross, he is terrified and remembers his greatest defeat and the loss of his labor and is therefore ashamed and runs away. Thus, all the sons of God constantly use the sign of the Cross, considering that it is the sign of conquest and victory–the power of God. As for our part, we are filled with power inside, but the enemy outside is scared.

As in ancient times, the bronze serpent was lifted up, as a healing for people and salvation from death, even so the Lord of glory was lifted up on the Cross (John 3:14). Thus is the sign of the Cross in its effect.

13. We make the sign of the Cross, and take its blessing.

In ancient times, the cross was a sign of curse and death because of sin, but on the Cross, the Lord bore all our evils, to grant us the benediction of the reconciliation with God (Romans 5:10), and the benediction of the new life. Therefore, all the gracious things of the New Testament come from the Cross.

Consequently, the members of the clergy use this cross while giving the benediction, as an indication that the benediction is not issued from them personally, but from the Cross of the Lord who has entrusted them to use it for granting benediction–for they take their ministry from the ministry of Him who was crucified. All the blessings of the New Testament follow the Cross of the Lord and its effect.

14. We use the Cross in all the Holy Mysteries of Christianity.

Since all the mysteries originate from the merits of the blood of Christ on the Cross, the Cross is an essential element in each of the holy mysteries. Without the Cross, we could not deserve to come near to God as sons in Baptism; and we could not deserve to partake of the Communion of His Body and Blood in the Mystery of Eucharist (1 Corinthians 11:26). Nor could we enjoy the blessings of any of the mysteries of the Church.

15. We pay attention to the Cross to remember our participation in it.

We remember the words of St. Paul the Apostle, "I have been crucified with Christ; it is no longer I who live, but Christ lives in me" (Galatians 2:20). We also remember his words, "that I may know Him and the power of His resurrection, and the fellowship of His sufferings, being conformed to His death" (Philippians 3:10). Here, we ask ourselves when shall we enter into participation with the sufferings of the Lord and be crucified with Him.

We also remember the thief who was crucified with Him, and deserved to be with Him in paradise. Probably, he is in Paradise singing with St. Paul, who said later "I have been crucified with Christ."

Our greatest wish is that we ascend on the Cross with Christ, and to boast about this Cross which we remember now whenever we touch it with our senses.

16. We honor the Cross, because it is a subject of joy for the Father.

The Father accepted Christ on the Cross with all joy, as a sin sacrifice and as "a burnt sacrifice, an offering made by fire, a sweet aroma to the Lord" (Leviticus 1:5, 13, 17).

The Lord Christ has satisfied the Father with the perfection of His life on earth, but He entered into the fullness of this satisfaction on the Cross, where He "became obedient to the point of death, even the death of the Cross" (Philippians 2:8).

Each time we look at the Cross, we remember the perfection of obedience, and the perfection of subjection, to imitate the Lord Christ in his obedience, to the point of death.

As the Cross was a subject of joy for the Father, so also it was a subject of joy regarding the Son Who was crucified. For it was said of Him: "Who for the joy that was set before Him endured the Cross, despising the shame" (Hebrews 12:2). Thus was the fullness of Christ's joy in His crucifixion. May we experience the same.

17. In the Cross, we also bear reproach.

In the Cross, "We go forth to Him outside the camp, bearing His reproach" (Hebrews 13:12) with the same feelings which we have in the Holy Week. In this, we remember what was said about the prophet Moses: "esteeming the reproach of Christ greater riches than the treasures in Egypt" (Hebrews 11:26). The reproach of Christ is His Crucifixion and His sufferings.

18. On the Cross, we remember salvation.

When looking to the Cross, we remember the thief on the right, who was crucified with the Lord and obtained salvation. This gives us a wonderful hope. How could a man be saved in the last hours of his life on earth, and get a promise to enter Paradise?

We remember how the Lord, with His spiritual influence on this thief, had been able to draw him to Himself. We remember the faith and confession of the thief, without remembering any of his previous sins. How great is that hope which was realized on the Cross!

19. The Cross reminds us of His Second Coming.

As it has been mentioned in the gospel about the end of the world and the Second Coming of our Lord: "Then the sign of the Son of Man will appear in heaven" [that is the Cross]...and they will see the Son of Man coming on the clouds" (Matthew 24:30). Let us remember the sign of the Son of Man on earth, so long as we expect this sign of His in heaven in His majestic coming.

The Cross in the Life of a Servant

The Cross is a symbol of suffering and three crosses symbolize three cases: The Cross of Christ is a symbol of suffering for righteousness' sake, while the other two crosses refer to suffering as a penalty for sin. These are divided into two kinds: one suffers because of his sins then repents and returns. The other suffers because of his sins but complains and grumbles, then dies in his sins. The cross which is for righteousness' sake is also of different kinds: The cross of love and sacrifice is like the Cross of Christ Who endured suffering to save us. "Greater love has no one than this, to lay down his life for his friends" (John 15:13).

There is another cross in offering. The greatest offering is that given from the needs where you prefer others to yourself. You become in need to let others take, like the widow who gave all that she had, her whole livelihood. Another cross is that of endurance: turning the other cheek and walking the second mile. It is not only bearing people's abuses, but being good to those who spitefully use you and loving them!

There is another cross in the spiritual struggle... in the victory of the spirit over the body, in enduring the hardships and wars of the world, the body and the devil. It is also in crucifying the body and its desires, having victory over oneself, and entering through the narrow gate. It is a cross to suffer for righteousness' sake. This is only for beginners. As for the perfect, the cross turns into joy and pleasure. We feel the narrowness of the gate at the beginning of the way but later on, we find pleasure in carrying out the commandment and loving it. By that time the way would not be distressful and what at first was a cross becomes a pleasure.

Martyrdom used to be a cross, then it turned out to be a pleasure. Saints began to desire martyrdom and long for death, and rejoice in it. Laboring and suffering for God's sake became a pleasure and an enjoyment. Therefore, the Bible considers suffering a gift from God: "For to you it has been granted on behalf of Christ, not only to believe in Him, but also to suffer for His sake" (Philippians 1:29).

When will the Cross be a joy in our life?

The Empress Helen and the Discovery of the Cross

The Coptic Orthodox Church remembers the life of St. Helen the Empress on three separate occasions:

✤ On 9 Bashans, (May 17), we commemorate her departure in the year 327.

✤ On the 17 Tout, (September 27 or 28), the day of the Feast of the Cross, we remember her role in finding of the Holy Cross in Jerusalem.

✤ The Church also remembers her in the chanting of the Commemoration of the Saints during the Holy Psalmody. In this prayer, the Church asks for her prayers and the prayers of her son the Emperor Constantine.

✤ Our brethren in the Greek Orthodox Church, build many churches after her name, and celebrate her feast with the feast of her son on the 21st of Ayar. The Latin Church celebrates her feast on 18 Aab (August).

Her son, Emperor Constantine, also honored her by giving her the surname "Augusta," which means "empress." He also gave her the power over the imperial treasures, which she spent generously and liberally on the construction of churches. She also gave to the poor and the needy persons and cities.

Eusebius of Caesarea, the historian, said that during her wandering in the eastern states, she presented numerous proofs of her magnanimity as empress. She bestowed her imperial generosity upon the inhabitants of the various cities, communities and upon the individuals with the utmost lavishness. She gave money to some, and large quantities of clothing to others. She liberated some from prisons and slavery in the mines. She delivered others from the violence of persecution and brought back some others from exile.

She was also very religious. She went to church, with simple modest clothes, although she was an empress, and she stood with all veneration among the masses. She was constant in her prayers, attended the religious celebrations, and lived as a worshipper more than she lived as an empress. She visited the holy places, and bore the fatigues of travel in her old age.

Then, the Lord suggested to her in a vision, to go to Jerusalem, and to search exactly for the place of the glorious Cross. Accompanied by St. Macarius, the bishop of Jerusalem, she traveled there, inquired, and discovered three crosses.

God manifested the holy Cross with a miracle, as it appears in the Synexarium on 17 Tout. She placed the Cross in a golden box, and gave it to the bishop, and she kept a part of it for her son Constantine, who placed some of the holy nails in his protective covering.

St. Helen then constructed several churches: one in Bethlehem, at the cave where our Lord was born; another at the Mount of Olives, where our Savior Ascended; and one at the tomb, where our Lord Resurrected.[2]

Her son, the Emperor Constantine, presented to her all that was necessary for her holy work. He sent letters concerning this to the governors and bishops. This saint specified numerous unalienable properties for the churches and the monasteries, and for spending on the poor. She celebrated a feast in Jerusalem for the sacred virgins, and she herself served them.

She built a church on the name of the martyr St. Lucianos in the town where she was born, which her son called Helenopolis on her name Helen, in her honor.

Then, she died in 327 AD at the age of 84. She wrote her testament to her son and grandsons the Caesars, inciting them to be firm in the life of faith and justice.

Verses from the Holy Scriptures about the Cross

✚ "I have been crucified with Christ; it is no longer I who live, but Christ lives in me" (Galatians 2:20).

---

[2] Constantine and Helen also built other churches such as the chapel at Mamre where Abraham was visited by the Lord Christ and two angels.

✤ "And those who are Christ's have crucified the flesh with its passions and desires" (Galatians 5:24).

✤ "But God forbid that I should boast except in the Cross of our Lord Jesus Christ, by Whom the world has been crucified to me, and I to the world" (Galatians 6:14).

✤ "For the Word of the Cross is foolishness to those who are perishing, but to us who are being saved it is the power of God" (1 Corinthians 1:18).

✤ "...having made peace through the blood of His Cross" (Colossians 1:20).

✤ "For I determined not to know anything among you except Jesus Christ and Him crucified" (1 Corinthians 2:2).

✤ "And whoever does not bear his cross and come after Me cannot be My disciple" (Luke 14:27).

✤ "Knowing this, that our old man was crucified with Him" (Romans 6:6).

✤ "For had they known, they would not have crucified the Lord of glory" (1 Corinthians 2:8).

❦ ✟ ❦

Historical Accounts of the Discovery of the Cross

✳

THE GREAT SEARCH

SOCRATES SCHOLASTICUS[1]

The emperor's mother, Helen, having come to Jerusalem, searches for and finds the Cross of Christ, and builds a Church.

H elen, the emperor's mother (from whose name having made Drepanum, once a village, a city, the emperor called it Helenopolis), being divinely directed by dreams went to Jerusalem. Finding that which was once Jerusalem, desolate "as a preserve for autumnal fruits" (Isaiah 1:8). According to the prophet, she sought carefully the sepulcher of Christ, from which He arose after His burial; and after much difficulty, by God's help she discovered it.

What the cause of the difficulty was I will explain in a few words. Those who embraced the Christian faith, after the period of His passion, greatly venerated this tomb; but those who hated Christianity, having covered the spot with a mound of earth, erected on it a temple to Venus, and set up her image there, not caring for the memory of the place. This succeeded for a long time, and it became known to the emperor's mother.

Accordingly, she having caused the statue to be thrown down, the earth to be removed, and the ground entirely cleared, found three crosses in the sepulcher: one of these was that blessed Cross on which Christ had hung, the other two were those on which the two thieves that were crucified with Him had died. With these was also found the tablet of Pilate, on which he had inscribed in various characters, that the Christ Who was crucified was King of the Jews.

Since, however, it was doubtful which was the Cross they were in search of, the emperor's mother was not a little distressed; but from this trouble the bishop of Jerusalem, Macarius, shortly

---

[1] Socrates Scholasticus, *Ecclesiastical History*, Book 1, Chapter 17, NPNF s. 2, v. 2.

relieved her. He solved the doubt by faith, for he sought a sign from God and obtained it. The sign was this: a certain woman of the neighborhood, who had been long afflicted with disease, was now just at the point of death; the bishop therefore arranged it so that each of the crosses should be brought to the dying woman, believing that she would be healed on touching the precious Cross.

Nor was he disappointed in his expectation: for the two crosses having been applied which were not the Lord's, the woman still continued in a dying state; but when the third, which was the true Cross, touched her, she was immediately healed, and recovered her former strength. In this manner then was the genuine Cross discovered.

The emperor's mother erected over the place of the sepulcher a magnificent church[2], and named it *New Jerusalem*, having built it facing that old and deserted city. There she left a portion of the Cross, enclosed in a silver case, as a memorial to those who might wish to see it: the other part she sent to the emperor, who being persuaded that the city would be perfectly secure where that relic should be preserved, privately enclosed it in his own statue, which stands on a large column of porphyry in the forum called Constantine's at Constantinople.

I have written this from report indeed; but almost all the inhabitants of Constantinople affirm that it is true.

Moreover the nails with which Christ's hands were fastened to the Cross (for his mother having found these also in the sepulcher had sent them) Constantine took and had made into bridle-bits and a helmet, which he used in his military expeditions. The emperor supplied all materials for the construction of the churches, and wrote to Macarius the bishop to expedite these edifices.

When the emperor's mother had completed the New Jerusalem, she reared another church not at all inferior, over the cave at Bethlehem where Christ was born according to the flesh:

---

[2] That is, "house of prayer."

nor did she stop here, but built a third on the mount of His Ascension. So devoutly was she affected in these matters, that she would pray in the company of women; and inviting the virgins enrolled in the register of the churches to a repast, serving them herself, she brought the dishes to table. She was also very generous to the churches and to the poor; and having lived a life of piety, she died when about eighty years old. Her remains were conveyed to New Rome[3], the capital, and deposited in the imperial sepulchers.

✳

CONSTANTINE'S COMMAND

THE HISTORIAN SOZOMEN[4]

C onstantine commands the sign of the Cross to be carried before him in battle; an extraordinary narrative about the bearers of the Sign of the Cross.

The emperor, amazed at the prophecies concerning Christ which were expounded to him by the priests, sent for some skillful artisans, and commanded them to remodel the standard called by the Romans Labarum, to convert it into a representation of the Cross, and to adorn it with gold and precious stones.

This warlike trophy was valued beyond all others; for it always used to be carried before the emperor, and was worshiped by the soldiers. I think that Constantine changed the most honorable symbol of the Roman power into the sign of Christ, chiefly that by the habit of having it always in view, and of worshiping it, the soldiers might be induced to abandon their ancient forms of superstition, and to recognize the true God, Whom the emperor worshiped, as their leader and their help in battle; for this symbol

---

[3] The title of "New Rome" was given to the city of Constantinople by the third canon of the Second Ecumenical Council of Constantinople in 381.

[4] Sozomen, *Ecclesiastical History*, Book I, Chapter 4, NPNF s. 1, v. 2.

was always borne in front of his own troops, and was, at the command of the emperor, carried among the phalanxes in the thickest of the fight by an illustrious band of spearmen, of whom each one in turn took the standard upon his shoulders, and paraded it through the ranks.

It is said that on one occasion, on an unexpected movement of the hostile forces, the man who held the standard in terror, placed it in the hands of another, and secretly fled from the battle. When he got beyond the reach of the enemy's weapons, he suddenly received a wound and fell, while the man who had stood by the divine symbol remained unhurt, although many weapons were aimed at him; for the missiles of the enemy, marvelously directed by divine agency, lighted upon the standard, and the bearer thereof, although in the midst of danger, was preserved.

❈

The Discovery of the Life-giving Cross and the Holy Nails

THE HISTORIAN SOZOMEN [5]

When the business at Nicaea had been transacted as above related, the priests returned home. The emperor rejoiced exceedingly at the restoration of unity of opinion in the Catholic Church, and desirous of expressing on behalf of himself, his children, and the empire, the gratitude towards God which the unanimity of the bishops inspired, he directed that a house of prayer should be erected to God at Jerusalem near the place called Calvary.

At the same time his mother Helen repaired to the city for the purpose of offering up prayer, and of visiting the sacred places. Her

---

[5] Sozomen, *Ecclesiastical History*, Book 2, Chapter 1, NPNF s. 1, v. 2.

zeal for Christianity made her eager to find the wood which had formed the adorable Cross.

But it was no easy matter to discover either this relic or the Lord's sepulcher; for the pagans, who in former times had persecuted the Church, and who, at the first promulgation of Christianity, had had recourse to every artifice to exterminate it, had concealed that spot under much heaped up earth, and elevated what before was quite depressed, as it looks now, and the more effectually to conceal them, had enclosed the entire place of the Resurrection and Mount Calvary within a wall, and had, moreover, ornamented the whole locality, and paved it with stone.

They also erected a temple to Aphrodite, and set up a little image, so that those who repaired there to worship Christ would appear to bow the knee to Aphrodite, and that thus the true cause of offering worship in that place would, in course of time, be forgotten; and that as Christians would not dare fearlessly to frequent the place or to point it out to others, the temple and statue would come to be regarded as exclusively appertaining to the pagans.

At length, however, the place was discovered, and the fraud about it so zealously maintained was detected. Some say that the facts were first disclosed by a Hebrew who dwelt in the East, and who derived his information from some documents which had come to him by paternal inheritance. But it seems more accordant with truth to suppose that God revealed the fact by means of signs and dreams; for I do not think that human information is requisite when God thinks it best to make manifest the same.

When by command of the emperor the place was excavated deeply, the cave in which our Lord arose from the dead was discovered; and at no great distance, three crosses were found and another separate piece of wood, on which were inscribed in white letters in Hebrew, in Greek, and in Latin, the following words: "Jesus of Nazareth, the King of the Jews." These words, as the sacred book of the gospels relates, were placed by command of Pilate, governor of Judaea, over the head of Christ.

There yet, however, remained a difficulty in distinguishing the Divine Cross from the others; for the inscription had been wrenched from it and thrown aside, and the Cross itself had been cast aside with the others, without any distinction, when the bodies of the crucified were taken down. For according to history, the soldiers found Jesus dead upon the Cross, and they took Him down, and gave Him up to be buried; while, to accelerate the death of the two thieves, who were crucified on either hand, they broke their legs, and then took down the crosses, and flung them out of the way.

It was no concern of theirs to deposit the crosses in their first order; for it was growing late, and as the men were dead, they did not think it worth while to remain to attend to the crosses. A more divine information than could be furnished by man was therefore necessary to distinguish the Divine Cross from the others, and this revelation was given in the following manner:

There was a certain woman of rank in Jerusalem who was afflicted with a most grievous and incurable disease; Macarius, bishop of Jerusalem, accompanied by the mother of the emperor and her attendants, repaired to her bedside. After engaging in prayer, Macarius signified by signs to the spectators that the Divine Cross would be the one which, on being brought in contact with the invalid, should remove the disease. He approached her in turn with each of the crosses; but when two of the crosses were laid on her, it seemed but folly and mockery to her for she was at the gates of death.

When, however, the third cross was in like manner brought to her, she suddenly opened her eyes, regained her strength, and immediately sprang from her bed, well. It is said that a dead person was, in the same way, restored to life. The venerated Wood having been thus identified, the greater portion of it was deposited in a silver case, in which it is still preserved in Jerusalem: but the empress sent part of it to her son Constantine, together with the nails by which the Body of Christ had been fastened.

Of these, it is related, the emperor had a headpiece and bit made for his horse, according to the prophecy of Zechariah, who referred to this period when he said, that "there shall be engraved on the bridle of every horse 'Holiness to the Lord Almighty'" (Zechariah 14:20, LXX). These things, indeed, were formerly known to the sacred prophets, and predicted by them, and at length, when it seemed to God that they should be manifested, were confirmed by wonderful works. Nor does this appear so marvelous when it is remembered that, even among the pagans, it was confessed that the Sibyl had predicted that thus it should be, "Oh most blessed tree, on which our Lord was hung."

❋

THE FEAST OF ENCAENIA

ST. EGERIA THE PILGRIM[6]

The date when the Church on Golgotha (called Martyrium) was consecrated to God is called Encaenia (cf. 2 Chronicles 7:5,9; John 10:22), and on the same day the Church of the Anastasis was also consecrated, the place where the Lord rose again after His Passion. The Encaenia of these holy churches is a feast of special significance, since it is on the very date when the Cross of the Lord was discovered. So they arranged that this day should be observed with all possible gladness by making the original dedication of these holy churches coincide with the very day when the Cross had been found. You will find in the Bible that the day of Encaenia was when the House of God was consecrated, and holy Solomon stood in prayer before the altar of God, as we read in the book of Chronicles [2 Chronicles 6:12].

At the time of Encaenia they keep festival for eight days, and for many days beforehand the crowds begin to assemble. Monks and apotactites come not only from the provinces having large

---

[6] *Egeria's Travels*, trans. John Wilkinson (2006), p. 164.

numbers of them such as Mesopotamia, Syria, Egypt and the Thebaid, but from every region and province. Not one of them fails to make for Jerusalem to share the celebrations of the solemn feast. There are also lay men and women from every province gathering in Jerusalem at the time, accompanied by many of their clergy. In fact, I should say, that people regard it as a grave sin to miss taking part in this solemn feast, unless anyone had been prevented from coming by an emergency.

The feast ranks with Easter or Epiphany, and during Encaenia they decorate the churches in the same way, and assemble each day in different holy places, as at Easter and Epiphany. On the first and second days they assemble in the Great Church, the Martyrium, on the third day in the Eleona Church on the Mount from which the Lord ascended into heaven after His Passion (I mean the church which contains the cave where the Lord taught the apostles on the Mount of Olives. On the fourth day...[7]

---

[7] The remaining pages are lost from the manuscript.

✥

THE WORD OF THE CROSS

✳

WHY THE CROSS?

ST. ATHANASIUS THE APOSTOLIC[1]

B ut if any honest Christian wants to know why He suffered death on the Cross and not in some other way, we answer thus: in no other way was it expedient for us, indeed the Lord offered for our sakes the one death that was supremely good.

2. For if He came Himself to bear the curse laid on us; and how could He "become a curse" (Galatians 3:13), otherwise than by accepting the accursed death? And that death is the Cross, for it is written, "Cursed is he who hangs on a tree" (Galatians 3:13).

3. Again, if the Lord's death is the ransom of all, and by His death "the middle wall of separation" (Ephesians 2:14) is broken down, and the calling of the nations is brought about, how could He have called us to Him, if He had not been crucified? For it is only on the Cross that a man dies with His arms outstretched. Thus it was fitting for the Lord to bear this also and to stretch out His arms: it was that He might draw His ancient people with the one and the Gentiles with the other, and to join both together in Himself.

4. For, this is what He Himself foretold the manner of His redeeming death. "And I, when I am lifted up from the earth, will draw all peoples to Myself" (John 12:32).

5. Again the air is the sphere of the devil, the enemy of our race, who having fallen from heaven, endeavors with the other evil spirits who shared in his disobedience both to keep souls from the truth and to hinder the progress of those who are trying to ascend it. The Apostle refers to this when he says: "According to the prince of the power of the air, of the spirit that now works in the sons of disobedience" (Ephesians 2:2). But the Lord came to

---

[1] St. Athanasius, *De Incarnatione*, 25, NPNF s. 2, v. 4.

overthrow the devil, to purify the air and to prepare "a way" for us up to heaven, as the apostle says, "through the veil, that is to say, His flesh" (Hebrews 10:20). This had to be done through death, and by what other kind of death could it be done, than by a death in the air, that is, on the Cross? Here again, you see how right and natural it was that the Lord should suffer for us.

6. For being thus "lifted up," He cleansed the air from all the evil influences of the enemy. "I beheld Satan as lightning fall from heaven" (Luke 10:18). He says; and thus He reopened the road to heaven, saying again, "Lift up your gates, O you princes, and be lifted up, you everlasting doors" (Psalms 24:7). For it was not the Word Himself Who needed an opening of the gates, He being Lord of all, nor was any of His works closed to their Maker. No, it was we that needed it, we whom He Himself carried up in His own Body–that Body which He first offered to death on behalf of all, and then made through it a path to heaven.

❈

THE ROAD OF THE CROSS

ST. ATHANASIUS THE APOSTOLIC[2]

Where our Lord Jesus Christ, Who took upon Him to die for all, stretched forth His hands, not somewhere on the earth beneath, but in the air itself, in order that the Salvation effected by the Cross might be shown to be for all men everywhere: destroying the devil who was working in the air: and that He might consecrate our road up to Heaven, and make it free.

---

[2] St. Athanasius, *Festal Letters,* 22.1 (350 AD).

※

OVERCOMING EVIL WITH GOOD

THE SCHOLAR ORIGEN[3]

G od does not create evil; nor does He prevent it when it is displayed by others, although He could do so. But He uses evil, and those who exhibit it, for necessary purposes. For by means of those in whom there is evil, He bestows honor and approval on those who strive for the glory of virtue.

Virtue, if unopposed, would not shine out nor become more glorious by probation. Virtue is not virtue if it be untested and unexamined...If you remove the wickedness of Judas and annul his treachery you take away likewise the Cross of Christ and His passion: and if there were no Cross then principalities and powers have not been stripped nor triumphed over by the wood of the Cross.

Had there been no death of Christ, there would certainly have been no resurrection and there would have been no "Firstborn from the dead" (cf. Colossians 1:18, Revelation 1:5) and then there would have been for us no hope of resurrection.

Similarly concerning the devil himself, if we suppose, for the sake of argument, that he had been forcibly prevented from sinning, or that the will to do evil had been taken away from him after his sin; then at the same time there would have been taken from us the struggle against the wiles of the devil, and there would be no crown of victory in store for him who rightly struggled.

---

[3] The Scholar Origen, *Contra Celsus*, 6.54.

✳

THE RAISED TEMPLE

ST. IGNATIUS OF ANTIOCH[4]

N ow, He suffered all these things for us; and He suffered them really, and not in appearance only, even as also He truly rose again. But not, as some of the unbelievers, who are ashamed of the formation of man, and the Cross, and death itself, affirm, that in appearance only, and not in truth, He took a body of the Virgin, and suffered only in appearance, forgetting, as they do, Him who said, "The Word became flesh" (John 1:14); and again, "Destroy this temple, and in three days I will raise it up" (John 2:19); and once more, "If I be lifted up from the earth, I will draw all men unto Me" (John 12:32). The Word therefore did dwell in flesh, for "Wisdom built herself a house" (Proverbs 9:1). The Word raised up again His own temple on the third day, when it had been destroyed by the Jews fighting against Christ. The Word, when His flesh was lifted up, after the manner of the brazen serpent in the wilderness, drew all men to Himself for their eternal salvation (Numbers 21:9; John 3:14).

✳

THE KING'S THRONE

THE SCHOLAR ORIGEN[5]

H e ruled as King through His suffering on the Cross.

---

[4] St. Ignatius, *Epistle to the Smyrnaeans*, Chapter 2: "Christ's True Passion," ANF v. 1.

[5] The Scholar Origen, *Commentary on Matthew*, 1.38.

✳

SEEK HIM ON THE CROSS

ST. ATHANASIUS THE APOSTOLIC[6]

L et us now keep the feast, my brethren, for as our Lord then gave notice to His disciples, so He now tells us beforehand, that "after some days is the Passover" (Matthew 26:2), in which the Jews indeed betrayed the Lord. But we celebrate His death as a feast, rejoicing because we then obtained rest from our afflictions. We are diligent in assembling ourselves together, for we were scattered in time past and were lost, and are found. We were far off, and are brought near. We were strangers, and have become His, Who suffered for us, and was nailed on the Cross, Who bore our sins, as the prophet says (Isaiah 53:4), and was afflicted for us, that He might put away from all of us grief, and sorrow, and sighing.

When we thirst, He satisfies us on the feast-day itself; standing and crying, "If any man thirst, let him come to Me, and drink" (John 7:37). For such is the love of the saints at all times, that they never once leave off, but offer the uninterrupted, constant sacrifice to the Lord, and continually thirst, and ask of Him to drink; as David chanted, "My God, my God, early will I seek You, my soul thirsts for You; many times my heart and flesh longs for You in a barren land, without a path, and without water. Thus was I seen by You in the sanctuary'" (Psalms 63:1, 2). And Isaiah the prophet says, "From the night my spirit seeks You early, O God, because Your commandments are light" (Isaiah 26:9). And another says, "My soul fainted for the longing it has for Your judgments at all times." And again he says, "For Your judgments I have hoped, and Your law will I keep at all times" (Psalms 118:20, 43, 44). Another boldly cries out, saying, "My eyes are ever towards the Lord" (Psalms 25:15). And with him one says, "The meditation of

---

[6] St. Athanasius, *Festal Letters*, 20.1 (348 AD).

my heart is before You at all times" (Psalms 19:14). Paul further advises, "At all times give thanks; pray without ceasing" (1 Thessalonians 5:17).

THE DEFEAT OF DEATH

ST. ATHANASIUS THE APOSTOLIC[7]

For that death is destroyed, and that the Cross is become the victory over it, and that it has no more power but is verily dead, this is no small proof, or rather an evident warrant, that it is despised by all Christ's disciples, and that they all take the aggressive against it and no longer fear it; but by the sign of the Cross and by faith in Christ tread it down as dead.

2. For of old, before the divine sojourn of the Savior took place, even to the saints death was terrible (cf. Psalms 55:4, 89:47; Job 18:14), and all wept for the dead as though they perished. But now that the Savior has raised His body, death is no longer terrible; for all who believe in Christ tread him under as nought, and choose rather to die than to deny their faith in Christ. For they verily know that when they die they are not destroyed, but actually [begin to] live, and become incorruptible through the Resurrection.

3. And that devil that once maliciously exulted in death, now that its pains were loosed (Acts 2:24), remained the only one truly dead. And a proof of this is, that before men believe Christ, they see in death an object of terror, and play the coward before him. But when they are gone over to Christ's faith and teaching, their contempt for death is so great that they even eagerly rush upon it, and become witnesses for the Resurrection the Savior has accomplished against it. For while still tender in years they make

[7] St. Athanasius, *De Incarnatione*, 27, NPNF s. 2, v. 4.

haste to die, and not men only, but women also, exercise themselves by bodily discipline against it. So weak has he become, that even women who were formerly deceived by him, now mock at him as dead and paralyzed.

4. For as when a tyrant has been defeated by a real king, and bound hand and foot, then all that pass by laugh him to scorn, buffeting and reviling him, no longer fearing his fury and barbarity, because of the king who has conquered him; so also, death having been conquered and exposed by the Savior on the Cross, and bound hand and foot, all they who are in Christ, as they pass by, trample on him, and witnessing to Christ scoff at death, jesting at him, and saying what has been written against him of old: "O death, where is your sting? O Hades, where is your victory?" (1 Corinthians 15:55).

※

THE KEY TO SALVATION

ST. IGNATIUS OF ANTIOCH[8]

L et my spirit be counted as nothing for the sake of the Cross, which is a stumbling-block to those that do not believe, but to us salvation and eternal life (cf. 1 Corinthians 1:18). The Cross of Christ is indeed a stumbling-block to those that do not believe, but to the believing it is salvation and life eternal. "Where is the wise man? Where the disputer?" (1 Corinthians 1:20). Where is the boasting of those who are called mighty? For the Son of God, Who was begotten before the ages, and established all things according to the will of the Father, He was conceived in the womb of Mary, according to the appointment of God, of the seed of David, and by the Holy Spirit. For says [the Scripture], "Behold, a virgin shall be with Child, and shall bring forth a Son, and He

---

[8] St. Ignatius, *Epistle to the Smyrnaeans*, Chapter 2: "Christ's True Passion," ANF v. 1.

shall be called Emmanuel" (Isaiah 7:14; Matthew 1:23). He was born and was baptized by John, that He might ratify the institution committed to that prophet.

✳

THE HEALING OF CREATION

ST. ATHANASIUS THE APOSTOLIC[9]

T he knowledge of our religion and of the truth of things is independently manifest rather than in need of human teachers, for almost day by day it asserts itself by facts, and manifests itself brighter than the sun by the doctrine of Christ.

2. Still, as you nevertheless desire to hear about it, Macarius, come let us as we may be able set forth a few points of the faith of Christ: able though you are to find it out from the divine oracles, but yet generously desiring to hear from others as well.

3. For although the sacred and inspired Scriptures are sufficient to declare the truth–while there are other works of our blessed teachers compiled for this purpose, if he meet with which a man will gain some knowledge of the interpretation of the Scriptures, and be able to learn what he wishes to know,–still, as we have not at present in our hands the compositions of our teachers, we must communicate in writing to you what we learned from them,–the faith, namely, of Christ the Savior; lest any should hold cheap the doctrine taught among us, or think faith in Christ unreasonable. For this is what the Gentiles traduce and scoff at, and laugh loudly at us, insisting on the one fact of the Cross of Christ; and it is just here that one must pity their want of sense, because when they traduce the Cross of Christ they do not see that its power has filled all the world, and that by it the effects of the knowledge of God are made manifest to all.

---

[9] St. Athanasius, *Contra Gentes*, 1.1, NPNF s. 2, v. 4.

4. For they would not have scoffed at such a fact, had they, too, been men who genuinely gave heed to His Divine Nature. On the contrary, they in their turn would have recognized this man as Savior of the world, and that the Cross has been not a disaster, but a healing of Creation.

5. For if after the Cross all idolatry was overthrown, while every manifestation of demons is driven away by this Sign, and Christ alone is worshipped and the Father known through Him, and, while gainsayers are put to shame, He daily invisibly wins over the souls of these gainsayers–how, one might fairly ask them, is it still open to us to regard the matter as human, instead of confessing that He Who ascended the Cross is Word of God and Savior of the World? But these men seem to me quite as bad as one who should traduce the sun when covered by clouds, while yet wondering at His Light, seeing how the whole of creation is illumined by Him.

6. For as the light is noble, and the sun, the chief cause of light, is nobler still, so, as it is a divine thing for the whole world to be filled with His knowledge, it follows that the orderer and chief cause of such an achievement is God and the Word of God.

7. We speak then as lies within our power, first refuting the ignorance of the unbelieving; so that what is false being refuted, the truth may then shine forth of itself, and that you yourself, friend, may be reassured that you have believed what is true, and in coming to know Christ have not been deceived. Moreover, I think it becoming to discourse to you, as a lover of Christ, about Christ, since I am sure that you rate faith in and knowledge of Him above anything else whatsoever.

❊

PLATO AND THE CROSS

ST. JUSTIN MARTYR[10]

A nd the physiological discussion concerning the Son of God in the Timaeus of Plato, where he says, "He placed him crosswise in the universe," he borrowed in like manner from Moses; for in the writings of Moses it is related how at that time, when the Israelites went out of Egypt and were in the wilderness, they fell in with poisonous beasts, both vipers and asps, and every kind of serpent, which slew the people; and that Moses, by the inspiration and influence of God, took brass, and made it into the figure of a cross, and set it in the holy tabernacle, and said to the people, "If when one bitten looks at this figure [and believes] you will be saved thereby" (Numbers 21:8).

And when this was done, it is recorded that the serpents died, and it is handed down that the people thus escaped death. Which things Plato reading, and not accurately understanding, and not apprehending that it was the figure of the Cross, but taking it to be a placing crosswise, he said that the power next to the first God was placed crosswise in the universe. And as to his speaking of a third, he did this because he read, as we said above, that which was spoken by Moses, "that the Spirit of God was hovering over the waters" (Genesis 1:2).

For he gives the second place to the Logos which is with God, who he said was placed crosswise in the universe; and the third place to the Spirit who was said to be borne upon the water, saying, "And the third around the third." And hear how the Spirit of prophecy signified through Moses that there should be a fire. He spoke thus: "Everlasting fire shall descend, and shall devour to the lowest hell" (Deuteronomy 32:22)

---

10 St. Justin Martyr, *Apology* 1.60, "Plato's Doctrine of the Cross," ANF v. 1.

It is not, then, that we hold the same opinions as others, but that all speak in imitation of ours. Among us these things can be heard and learned from persons who do not even know the forms of the letters, who are uneducated and barbarous in speech, though wise and believing in mind; some, indeed, even maimed and deprived of eyesight; so that you may understand that these things are not the effect of human wisdom, but are uttered by the power of God.

※

THE DOOR OF THE CROSS

ST. ATHANASIUS THE APOSTOLIC[11]

For it is God, my beloved, even the God Who at first established the feast for us, Who promises the celebration of it year by year. He both brought about the slaying of His Son for salvation, and gave us this reason for the holy feast, to which every year bears witness, as often as at this season the feast is proclaimed. This also leads us on from the Cross through this world to that which is before us, and God produces even now from it the joy of glorious salvation, bringing us to the same assembly, and in every place uniting all of us in spirit; appointing us common prayers, and a common grace proceeding from the feast. For this is the marvel of His loving-kindness, that He should gather together in the same place those who are at a distance; and make those who appear to be far off in the body, to be near together in unity of spirit.

---

[11] Saint Athanasius, *Festal Letters*, 5.2 (333 AD).

✳

THE SIGN OF HIS COMING

ST. CYRIL OF JERUSALEM[12]

B ut the Lord, Who shall come from heaven on the clouds, is
He Who ascended on the clouds; for He Himself has said,
"And they shall see the Son of Man coming on the clouds of
heaven, with power and great glory" (Matthew 24:30). But, what is
the sign of His coming, lest a hostile power dare to counterfeit it?
"And then shall appear, He says, the sign of the Son of Man in
heaven" (Matthew 24:30).

Now Christ's own true sign is the Cross; a sign of a luminous
Cross shall go before the King, plainly declaring Him who was
formerly crucified: that the Jews who before pierced Him and
plotted against Him, when they see it, may mourn tribe by tribe,
saying: "This is He Who was struck, this is He Whose face they
spat on, this is He Whom they bound with chains, this is He
Whom of old they crucified, and despised. "Where," they will say,
"shall we flee from the face of Your wrath?" But the angelic hosts
shall encompass them, so that they shall not be able to flee
anywhere.

The Sign of the Cross shall be a terror to His foes; but joy to
His friends who have believed in Him, or preached Him, or
suffered for His sake.

Who then is the happy man, who shall then be found a friend
of Christ? That King, so great and glorious, attended by the
angelic guards, the partner of the Father's throne, will not despise
His own servants.

For in order that His Elect may not be confused with His
foes, He shall send forth His angels with a great trumpet, and they
shall gather together His elect from the four winds. He did not

---

12 St. Cyril of Jerusalem, *Catechetical Lecture* 15, §§21-22, NPNF s. 2, v. 7.

despise Lot, who was but one; how then shall He despise many righteous? "Come, you blessed of My Father," will He say to those who shall then ride on chariots of clouds, and be assembled with Angels.

❋

DO NOT BE ASHAMED OF THE CROSS

THE SCHOLAR ORIGEN[13]

P aul knew of [Him when] he said to the Corinthians, "I determined not to know anything among you except Jesus Christ and Him crucified" (1 Corinthians 2:2). Therefore, formerly [the disciples] proclaimed Jesus as the doer of certain things, and the teacher of certain things; but now when Peter confesses that He was the Christ, the Son of the living God, as He did not wish it to be proclaimed already that He was the Christ, in order that He might be proclaimed at a more suitable time, and that as crucified, He commands His disciples that they should tell no man that He was the Christ.

And that this was His meaning, when He forbade proclamation to be made that He was the Christ, is in a measure established by the words, "From that time Jesus began to show to His disciples how He must go to Jerusalem, and suffer many things from the elders" (Matthew 16:21), and what is annexed; for then, at the fitting time, He proclaims, so to speak, to the disciples who knew that Jesus was Christ, the Son of the living God, the Father having revealed it to them, that instead of believing in Jesus Christ Who had been crucified, they were to believe in Jesus Christ Who was about to be crucified.

But also, instead of believing in Christ Jesus and Him risen from the dead, He teaches them to believe in Christ Jesus and

---

[13] The Scholar Origen, *Second Book on the Commentary on Matthew*, Book 12.18, ANF v. 10.

Him about to be risen from the dead. But since "having disarmed principalities and powers, He made a public spectacle of them, triumphing over them in the Cross" (Colossians 2:15).

If any one is ashamed of the Cross of Christ, he is ashamed of the dispensation on account of which these powers were triumphed over; and it is fitting that he, who both believes and knows these things, should glory in the cross of our Lord Jesus Christ, through which, when Christ was crucified, the principalities–among which, I think, was also the prince of this world–were made a show of and triumphed over before the believing world. Wherefore, when His suffering was at hand he said, "Now the ruler of this world is judged" (John 16:11); and, "Now shall the prince of this world will be cast out" (John 12:32), and, "I, if I am lifted from the earth, will draw all peoples to Myself" (John 12:32), since [the devil] no longer had sufficient power to prevent those going to Jesus who were being drawn by Him.

❊

SATAN'S GREAT DEFEAT

ST. EPHREM THE SYRIAN[14]

B ehold! Death was prompt beforehand, to mock Satan: him who was doomed to become a mockery at the last.

2. Refrain: Glory to You Who by Your Crucifixion, did conquer the Evil One: and by Your resurrection gain victory, likewise over Death!

3. And for our Lord's sake Death spoke curses on him: who was the cause of His shame, and Crucifixion.

4. Death: The fiery pit be your grave, O Satan: who blasphemed the Voice from the grave, that rent the graves

---

[14] St. Ephrem the Syrian, *Nisibine Hymns*, No. 57, NPNF s. 2, v. 13.

5. My Lord I know, and the Son of my Lord, O you Satan! You have denied your Lord, and crucified the Son of your Lord.

6. This is the name that fits you, "Slayer of your Lord": when He appears Whom you slew, He shall slay you.

7. At you shall every one shake the head, for by you the chiefs: shook their heads at Him, the Lord of life.

8. A bruised reed under the feet, of the just shall you be: for through you they put a reed in His hand, Who upholds all.

9. With a crown of thorns was He crowned, to signify: that He took the diadem of the kingdom, of the house of David.

10. With a crown of thorns was He crowned, the King of kings: but He took the diadem of the king, of those who shamed Him.

11. In the robes of mockery that they gave Him, in those He mocked them: for He took the raiment of glory, of priests and kings.

12. To vinegar is your memory akin, O you Satan: who offered vinegar for the thirst, of the Fount of Life.

13. The hand shall every man lift against you who strengthened the hand that smote Him by Whose hand, all creatures stand.

14. He was smitten by the hand and He cut off the hand, of Caiaphas: the hand of the priesthood is cut off, in the cutting off of the unction.

15. On the pillar again they stretched Him, as for scourging: Him Whose pillar went before, to guide their tribes.

16. The pillar on the pillar, He was scourged: He removed Himself from out of Zion, and its fall came.

17. When they put two beams together, to form the Cross: He broke them, even the two staves, the guardians of them.

18. Ezekiel put together the sticks, the two in one: in the two beams of the Cross, their staves have ceased.

19. The two sticks, as it were wings, bore the people: lo! his two planks were broken, even as his wings.

20. The bosom and wings of the Cross, He opened in mercy: its wings bowed and bore the nations, to go to Eden.

21. It is akin to the Tree of Life, and unto the son of its stock: it leads its beloved that on its branches, they may feed on its fruits.

22. Go howl and weep, Evil One, for me and for you: for not one of us shall enter the "Garden of Life."

23. Supplication: Now that you have confessed O Death, come let me tell you: that all this discourse of yours, to me is idle talk.

24. I will go and watch the snares, which I have set: you too, Death, fly and look after, all that are sick.

25. Our Lord has brought both to nought, on either hand: the Evil One shall be brought to nought here, and Death hereafter there.

❅

SHED YOUR TEARS TODAY

ST. EPHREM THE SYRIAN[15]

I am afraid to speak and touch with my tongue this fearful narrative concerning the Savior. For truly it is fearful to

---

[15] This sermon on the Passion is one of the metrical texts in Greek attributed to St Ephrem the Syrian. It is written in heptasyllabics, known in Syriac as the meter of St Ephrem. This text was translated by the text published in Thessaloniki by K.G Phrantzolas in 1988. This text is slightly amended in order to restore the meter. The text displays a number of interesting linguistic features, including one word that appears to attested nowhere else in Greek. One of the most interesting passages in the poem is that which describes the Holy Spirit as having come forth in the form of a dove and rent the veil of the Temple at the moment of the Lord's death—unique idea in patristic literature. This is the first known translation of English.

narrate all this.

Our Lord was given up today into the hands of sinners!

For what reason then was One Who is holy and without sin given up? For having done no sin He was given up today. Come, let us examine closely why Christ our Savior was given up.

For us, the ungodly, the Master was given up. Who would not marvel? Who would not give glory?

When the slaves had sinned the Master was given up.

The sons of perdition and the children of darkness went out in the darkness to arrest the Sun who had the power to consume them in an instant.

But the Master, knowing their insolence and the force of their anger, with gentleness, by His own authority, gave Himself up into the hands of the ungodly. And lawless men, having bound, the most pure Master, mocked the one who had bound the strong one with unbreakable bonds, and set us free from the bonds of sins.

They plaited a crown of their own thorns; the fruit borne by the vine of the Jews. In mockery they called Him 'King.' The lawless spat in the face of the most pure, at Whose glance all the Powers of heaven and the ranks of Angels quake with fear.

See, once again grief and tears grip hold of my heart, as I contemplate the Master enduring outrage and insults, scourgings, spitting from slaves, and blows. Come, observe well the abundance of compassion, the forbearance and mercy of our sweet Master.

He had a useful slave in the Paradise of delight, and when he sinned he was given to the torturers. But when the Good One saw his weakness of soul He took compassion on the slave and had mercy on him and presented Himself to be scourged by him.

I wished to remain silent because my mind was utterly amazed; but then again I was afraid lest I reject by my silence my Savior's grace. For my bones tremble when I think of it. The Creator of all things, our Lord Himself, was today arraigned before

Caiaphas, like one of the condemned; and one of the servants struck Him a blow.

My heart trembles as I think on these things: the slave is seated, the Master stands; and one full of iniquities passes sentence, on the One Who is sinless. The heavens trembled, earth's foundations shuddered; angels and archangels all quailed with terror. Gabriel and Michael covered their faces with their wings. The Cherubim at the throne were hidden beneath the wheels; The Seraphim struck their wings one with the other at that moment, when a servant gave a blow to the Master.

How did earth's foundations endure the earthquake and the tremor at that moment, when the Master was outraged?

I observe and I tremble and again I am stunned, when I see the long-suffering of the loving Master. For see my inward parts tremble as I speak, because the Creator, Who by grace fashioned humanity from dust, He the Fashioner is struck.

Let us fear, my brethren and not simply listen. The Savior endured all these things for us. Wretched servant, tell us why you struck the Master? All servants, when they are set free, receive a blow, that they may obtain freedom that perishes; but you, miserable wretch, unjustly gave a blow to the Liberator of all.

Did you perhaps expect to receive from Caiaphas a reward for your blow? Had you perhaps not heard, had you perhaps not learned that Jesus is the heavenly Master? You gave a blow to the Master of all things, but became slave of slaves to age on age, a disgrace and abomination, and condemned forever in unquenchable fire.

A great marvel, brethren, it is to see the gentleness of Christ the King struck by a slave! He answered patiently, with gentleness and all reverence.

A servant is indignant, the Master endures; a servant is enraged, the Master is kind. At a time of anger, who could endure rage and disturbance? But our Lord submitted to all this by His goodness.

Who can express Your long-suffering, O Master? You who are longed for and loved by Christ, draw near, with compunction and longing for the Savior. Come, let us learn what took place today in Zion, David's city.

The longed-for and chosen offspring of Abraham, What did they do today? They gave up to death the most pure Master on this day. Christ our Savior was unjustly hanged on the tree of the Cross through lawless hands.

Come, let us all wash our bodies with tears and groans, because our Lord, the King of glory, for us ungodly people was given up to death.

If someone suddenly hears of one truly Beloved having died, or again, suddenly sees the Beloved Himself lying a dead corpse before their eyes, their appearance is altered, and the brightness of their sight is darkened.

So, in heaven's height, when it saw the outrage to the Master on the tree of the Cross, the bright sun's appearance was altered; it withdrew the rays of its own brightness, and unable to look on the outrage to the Master, clothed itself in grief and darkness.

Likewise the Holy Spirit, Who is in the Father, when He saw the beloved Son on the tree of the Cross, rending the veil, the temple's adornment, suddenly came forth in the form of a dove.

All creation was in fear and trembling, when the King of heaven, the Savior suffered; while we sinners for whom the only Immortal was given up ever treat this with contempt!

We laugh each day when we hear of the Savior's sufferings and outrage. We enjoy ourselves daily, filled with great zeal to deck ourselves in fine clothing.

The sun in the sky because of the outrage to its Master changed its radiance into darkness, so that we, when we saw it, might follow its example. The Master on the Cross was outraged for your sake, while you, miserable wretch, ever deck yourself in splendid raiment.

Does your heart not tremble, does your mind not quail, when you hear such things? The One Who alone is sinless was for you given over to a shameful death, to outrages and revilings, while you hear all this with lofty indifference.

The whole rational flock should look intently on its Shepherd, and ever long for Him and respect Him, because for its sake He suffered, He the Impassable and all pure. Nor should it deck itself in corruptible garments, nor yet indulge in pleasure and worldly nourishment, but should give its Maker pleasure by ascesis and true reverence.

Let us not become imitators of the Jews; a people harsh and disobedient and that ever rejects the blessings and benefactions of God. God Most High, for the sake of Abraham and his covenant, from the beginning bore the stubbornness of the people.

From heaven He gave them Manna to eat; but they, the unworthy, longed for garlic, evil-smelling foods (cf. Numbers 11:15). Again, He gave them water from the rock in the desert; while they in place of these gave Him vinegar when they hanged Him on a Cross.

Let us be careful, brethren, not to be found as fellows of the Jews who crucified the Master, their own Creator. Let us always be fearful, keeping before our eyes the Savior's sufferings.

Let us always keep in mind His sufferings, because it was for us He suffered, the dispassionate Master; for us He was crucified, the only sinless One.

What return can we make for all this, brethren?

Let us be attentive to ourselves and not despise His sufferings. Draw near all of you, children of the Church, bought with the precious and holy Blood of the most pure Master. Come, let us meditate on His sufferings with tears, thinking on fear, meditating with trembling, saying to ourselves, 'Christ our Savior, for us the impious, was given over to death.'

Learn well, brother, what it is you hear: God Who is without sin, Son of the Most High, for you was given up. Open your heart, learn in detail His sufferings and say to yourself:

God who is without sin
today was given up,
today was mocked,
today was abused,
today was struck,
today was scourged,
today wore a crown of thorns,
today was crucified,
He, the heavenly Lamb.

Your heart will tremble, your soul will shudder.

Shed tears every day by this meditation on the Master's sufferings. Tears become sweet, the soul is enlightened that always meditates on Christ's sufferings.

Always meditating thus, shedding tears every day, giving thanks to the Master for the sufferings that He suffered for you, so that in the day of His Coming your tears may become your boast and exaltation before the Judgement Seat.

Endure as you meditate on the loving Master's sufferings, endure temptations, give thanks from your soul.

Blessed is the one who has before his eyes the heavenly Master and His sufferings, and has crucified himself from all the passions and earthly deeds, who has become an imitator of his own Master. This is understanding; this is the attitude of servants who love God, when they become ever imitators of their Master by good works.

Shameless man, do you watch the most pure Master hanging on the Cross, while you pass the time that you have to live on earth in pleasure and laughter? Don't you know, miserable wretch, that the crucified Lord will demand an account of all your disdainful deeds, for which, when you hear of them, you show no concern, and as you take your pleasure you laugh and enjoy yourself with indifference?

The day will come, that fearful day, for you to weep unceasingly and cry out in the fire from your pains, and there will be no one at all to answer and have mercy on your soul.

I worship you, Master;
I bless You, O Good One;
I entreat You, O Holy One;
I fall down before You, Lover of mankind;
and I glorify You, O Christ,

Because You, Only-Begotten, Master of all, and alone without sin, for me the unworthy sinner were given over to death, death on a Cross, that You might free the sinner's soul from the bonds of sins.

And what shall I give You in return for this, Master?

Glory to You, Lover of humankind!
Glory to You, O Merciful!
Glory to You, O Long-suffering!
Glory to You, Who pardon every fault!
Glory to You, Who came down to save our souls!
Glory to You, incarnate in the Virgin's womb!
Glory to You, Who were bound!
Glory to You, Who were scourged!
Glory to You, Who were crucified!
Glory to You, Who were buried!
Glory to You, Who were raised!
Glory to You, Who were proclaimed!
Glory to You, Who were believed!
Glory to You, Who were taken up!

Glory to You, Who were enthroned with great glory at the Father's right hand, and are coming again with the glory of the Father and the holy Angels to judge every soul that has despised Your holy sufferings in that dreadful and fearful hour;

When the powers of heaven will be shaken; when Angels, Archangels, Cherubim and Seraphim will come all together with fear and trembling before Your glory;

When all the foundations of the earth will tremble, and everything that has breath will shudder at Your great and unendurable glory.

In that hour Your hand will hide me under its wings and my soul be delivered from the fearful fire, the gnashing of teeth, the outer darkness and unending weeping, that blessing You, I may say:

"Glory to the One, Who wished to save the sinner through the many acts of pity of his compassion."

§ ✛ ᒃ

THE CROSS
IN THE OLD TESTAMENT

❊

THE HIDDEN CROSS

THE SCHOLAR TERTULLIAN[1]

C oncerning the last step, plainly, of His passion you raise a doubt; affirming that the passion of the Cross was not predicted with reference to Christ, and urging, besides, that it is not credible that God should have exposed His own Son to that kind of death; because Himself said, "Cursed is every one who shall hang on a tree" (Deuteronomy 21:23; Galatians 3:13). But the reason of the case antecedently explains the sense of this curse; for He says in Deuteronomy: "Moreover, if a man shall commit some sin incurring the judgment of death, and shall die, and you shall hang him on a tree, his body shall not remain on the tree overnight, but you shall bury him that very day; because cursed by God is every one who is hanged on a tree; and you shall not defile the land which the Lord your God gives you as an inheritance" (Deuteronomy 21:22, 23).

Therefore, He did not adjudge Christ to this passion by a curse, but drew a distinction, that whoever, in any sin, had incurred the judgment of death, and died suspended on a tree, he should be "cursed by God," because his own sins were the cause of his suspension on the tree. On the other hand, Christ, Who spoke not guile from His mouth (1 Peter 2:22; Isaiah 53:9), and who exhibited all righteousness and humility, not only (as we have above recorded it predicted of Him) was not exposed to that kind of death for His own failures, but [was so exposed] in order that what was predicted by the prophets as destined to come upon Him through your means might be fulfilled.

Just as in the Psalms, the Spirit of Christ Himself was already singing, saying, "They repaid me evil for good" (Psalms 34:12); "What I had not seized I was paying in full" (Psalms 68:5); "They

---

[1] The Scholar Tertullian, *An Answer the Jews*, Ch. 10, ANF v. 3.

pierced My hands and My feet" (Psalms 21:17); "They gave me gall for My food, and they gave Me vinegar for My drink" (Psalms 68:22); and "For My clothing they cast lots" (Psalms 21:19). Likewise, the other [outrages] which you committed against Him were foretold–all which He actually and thoroughly suffered not for any evil action of His own, but "that the Scriptures from the mouth of the prophets might be fulfilled" (cf. Matthew 26:56; 27: 34, 35; John 19:23, 24, 28, 32-37).

And, of course, it had been meet that the Mystery of the Passion itself should be figuratively set forth in predictions; and the more incredible [that mystery], the more likely to be "a stumbling-stone" (cf. Romans 9:32,33; Isaiah 28:16; 1 Corinthians 1:23; Galatians 5:11) if it had been openly predicted; and the more magnificent, the more to be foreshadowed, that the difficulty of its intelligence might seek (help from) the grace of God.

Accordingly, to begin with, Isaac, when led by his father as a victim, and himself bearing his own "wood"[2] was even at that early period pointing to Christ's death; conceded, as He was, as a victim by the Father; carrying, as He did, the "wood" of His own passion (Genesis 22:1–10; John 19:17).

Joseph, again, himself was made a type of Christ in this point alone (to name no more, not to delay my own course), that he suffered persecution at the hands of his brethren, and was sold into Egypt, on account of the favor of God (Genesis 37); just as Christ was sold by Israel–(and therefore) "according to the flesh," by His "brethren" (Romans 9:5)–when He is betrayed by Judas.[3] Joseph is, moreover, blessed by his father[4] after this form: "His glory [is that] of a bull; his horns, the horns of a unicorn; on them shall he toss

---

[2] *Xylon* in Greek (*Lignum* in Latin) is used often "tree."

[3] Alternatively, "Judah."

[4] As indicated above, this blessing is not included in Jacob's blessing of Joseph, recorded in Deuteronomy 33:13-17, but the Psalmist.

nations alike unto the very extremity of the earth" (cf. Psalms 91:11).

Of course no one-horned rhinoceros was there pointed to, nor any two-horned minotaur. But Christ was therein signified as the "bull" by reason of each of His two characters: to some (He is) fierce as Judge; to others gentle as Savior. His "horns" were to be the extremities of the Cross. For even in a ship's yard–which is part of a cross–this is the name by which the extremities are called. Also, the central pole of the mast is a "unicorn." By this power, in fact, of the Cross, and in this manner horned, He does now, on the one hand, "toss" universal nations through faith, wafting them away from earth to heaven; and will one day, on the other, "toss" them through judgment, casting them down from heaven to earth.

He, again, will be the bull elsewhere else in the same Scripture (cf. Genesis 29:5-7). When Jacob pronounced a blessing on Simeon and Levi, he prophesies of the scribes and Pharisees; for from them is derived their origin.[5] For [his blessing] interprets spiritually thus: "Simeon and Levi perfected iniquity out of their sect," (cf. Genesis 34:25-31)–whereby they persecuted Christ: "into their counsel come not my soul! and upon their station rest not my heart! because in their indignation they slew men"–that is, prophets–"and in their self will they hamstrung a bull!" (cf. Genesis 49:6)[6]–that is, Christ, Whom they slew after the slaughter of prophets and exhausted their savagery by transfixing His sinews with nails. Else it is idle if, after the murder already committed by them, he upbraids others, and not them, with butchery.

But, let us come now to Moses. Why, I wonder, did he merely pray sitting with hands extended at the time when Joshua was battling against Amalek? For, in circumstances so critical, he should have rather commended his prayer with knees bended, hands beating his breast, and a face prostrate on the ground. However, it was that there, where the name of the Lord Jesus was

---

[5] That is, from Simon and Levi, come the scribes and Pharisees.

[6] Compare with LXX, which often reads "ox" (tau`ron).

the theme of speech. Just He was destined to enter the lists one day alone against the devil, the figure of the Cross was also necessary, (that figure) through which Jesus was to win the victory (cf. Exodus 17:8–16; Colossians 2:14, 15).

Why, again, did the same Moses, after the prohibition (not to make) the "likeness of anything," (Exodus 20:4) set forth a brazen serpent, placed on a "tree," in a hanging posture, for a spectacle of healing to Israel, at the time when, after their idolatry,[7] they were suffering extermination by serpents? By doing so, he was only exhibiting the Lord's Cross on which the "serpent" the devil was "made a public spectacle of," (cf. Colossians 2:14, 15; Genesis 3:1; 2 Corinthians 11:3; Revelation 13:9). For every person hurt by such snakes–that is, his angels (cf. 2 Corinthians 11:14, 15; Matthew 25:41; Revelation 12:9)–after turning intently from the offense of sins to the sacraments of Christ's cross, will work out salvation. For he who gazed then upon that (Cross) was freed from the bite of the serpents.

Come, now, if you have read in the utterance of the prophet in the Psalms, "God has reigned from the tree," (Psalms 95:10).[8] I wait to hear what you understand thereby. For perhaps you might think some carpenter-king[9] is signified, and not Christ, Who has reigned from that time onward when He overcame the death which ensued from His passion of "the tree."

---

[7] The sin of Israel was *"speaking against God and Moses"* (Numbers 21:4–9).

[8] Although the words "from the tree" are not included in many translations, this text is present in many Greek and Coptic manuscripts of Psalm 95:10. Its often citation by the Fathers of the Church hints to a possible corruption of the text by later Jewish sources. Moreover, the Coptic Church places this psalm as the first to be prayed in the Ninth Hour, commemorating the Lord's Death on the Cross, the time of His true reign over death, the world, and sin, "trampling death by death" and swallowing up death's power in the Victory of the Resurrection (cf. 1 Corinthians 15:54-57).

[9] Likewise, our Lord is not only called by the Jews *"the carpenter's son"* (Matthew 13: 55; Luke 4:22), but *"the carpenter"* (Mark 6:3).

Similarly, again, Isaiah says: "For unto us a Child is born, unto us a Son is given" (Isaiah 9:5, LXX). What novelty is that, unless he is speaking of the "Son" of God? For this One born to us is the beginning of whose government has been placed "on His shoulder." What king in the world wears the ensign of his power on his shoulder, and does not bear either diadem on his head, or else scepter in his hand, or else some mark of distinctive vesture? But the novel "King of ages," Christ Jesus, alone reared "on His shoulder" His own novel glory, and power, and sublimity–the Cross, such that, according to the former prophecy, the Lord thus "might reign from the tree."

For of this tree likewise it is that God hints, through Jeremiah, that you would say, "Come, let us put wood into his bread, and let us wear him away out of the land of the living; and his name shall no more be remembered" (Jeremiah 11:19). Of course on His body that "wood" was put.[10] Christ has also revealed this by calling His body "bread," whose body the prophet in earlier days announced under the term "bread."

If you shall still seek for predictions of the Lord's Cross, the twenty-first Psalm will at length be able to satisfy you, containing as it does the whole passion of Christ; singing, as He does, even at so early a date, His own glory. "They nailed," He says, "My hands and feet" (Psalm 21:17)–which is the peculiar atrocity of the Cross. Again, when He implores the aid of the Father, "Save me," He says, "out of the mouth of the lion"–of course, of death–"and from the horns of the unicorns my humility," (v. 22)–from the ends, of the Cross, as we have shown above. Such a cross neither David himself suffer, nor any of the kings of the Jews: so that you may not think the passion of some other particular man is here prophesied than His who alone was so signally crucified by the People.

Now, if the hardness of your heart shall persist in rejecting and deriding all these interpretations, we will prove that it may suffice

---

[10] That is, when they laid on Him the crossbeam to carry (cf. John 19:17).

that the death of the Christ had been prophesied. This was done so that we may understand that because the nature of the death had not been specified, it had been affected by means of the Cross; likewise, the passion of the Cross is not to be ascribed to anyone but Him Whose death was constantly being predicted.

For I desire to show, in one utterance of Isaiah, His death, and passion, and burial. "Because of the lawlessness," he says, "for My people He was led to death; and I will appoint evil men for His burial, and rich men for His death, because He did no wickedness, nor was deceit found in His mouth; and God willed to cleanse His soul from death" (Isaiah 53:8-10). He says again, moreover: "His burial shall be taken away from the midst" (Isaiah 57:2). For neither was He buried except He were dead, nor was His sepulture removed from the midst except through His resurrection. Finally, he adds, "Therefore He shall have many for an inheritance, and of many shall He divide spoils" (Isaiah 53:12). For who else [shall so do] but He who "was born," as we have shown above, so that His soul may be delivered unto death?

For, the cause of the favor accorded Him being shown–in return, such that for the injury of a death which had to be recompensed–it is likewise shown that He, destined to attain these rewards because of death, was to attain them after death, of course after Resurrection. For that which happened at His passion, that midday grew dark, the prophet Amos announces, saying, "And it shall be," he says, "in that day, says the Lord, the sun shall set at noon, and the day of light shall grow dark over the land: and I will turn your feasts into mourning, and all your canticles into lamentation; and I will lay upon your loins sackcloth, and upon every head baldness; and I will make the grief like that for a Beloved [Son], and those who are with Him like a day of mourning" (Amos 8:9, 10).

For that you would do thus at the beginning of the first month of your new [years] even Moses prophesied, when he was foretelling that all the community of the sons of Israel was to roast a lamb at evening, and they were to eat this solemn sacrifice of this day (that is, of the Passover of unleavened bread) with "bitterness;" and added that "it was the Lord's Pascha" (Exodus 12:11), that is, the Pascha of Christ. Thus, this prophesy was also fulfilled, for "on the first day of unleavened bread" (cf. Matthew 26:17; Mark 14:12; Luke 22:7; John 18:28) you slew Christ (1 Corinthians 5:7). And so (that the prophecies might be fulfilled) the day hastened to make an "evening,"–that is, to cause darkness, which was made at noon; and thus God turned "your feasts into mourning, and all your canticles into lamentation." For after the passion of Christ there overtook you even captivity and dispersion, predicted before through the Holy Spirit.

❋

PROPHESIES OF THE CROSS

ST. ATHANASIUS THE APOSTOLIC[11]

B ut, perhaps, having heard the prophecy of His death, you ask to learn also what is set forth concerning the Cross. For not even this is passed over: it is displayed by the holy men with great plainness.

2. For first Moses predicts it, and that with a loud voice, when he says: "You Life shall hang before your eyes, and you shall fear day and night" (Deuteronomy 28:66),

3. And next, the prophets after him witness of this, saying: "But I as an innocent Lamb brought to the slaughter, and I did not know that they had devised schemes against Me, saying, 'Come and let us cast a tree upon His bread, and let us cut Him off from the land of the living'" (Jeremiah 11:18).

4. And again: "They pierced My hands and My feet, I numbered all My bones...they divided My garments among them, and for My clothing they cast lots" (Psalms 21:17-19).

---

[11] St. Athanasius, *De Incarnatione*, §35.

St. Michael's Abbey Lent Prayer List 2011

Fr. Abbot Eugene J. Hayes

Fr. Prior Hugh C. Barbour

Fr. Subprior James G. Smith

Fr. Rector Stephen M. Boyle

Fr. Thomas W. Nelson

Fr. Gerlac A. Horvath

Fr. Robert S. Hodges

Fr. Leo J. Celano

Fr. Martin Benzoni

Fr. Joseph K. Horn

Fr. Bernard M. Johnson

Fr. Norbert J. Wood

Fr. Gabriel D. Stack

Fr. Hildebrand J. Garceau

Fr. Philip T. Smith

Fr. Raymond L. Perez

Fr. Michael U. Perea

Fr. Theodore R. Smith

Fr. Vincent M. Gilmore

Fr. Francis M. Gloudeman

Fr. Anthony J. Kopp

Fr. Peter Muller

Fr. Patrick D. Foutts

Fr. Jerome M. Molokie

Fr. John E. Caronan

Fr. Paschal B. Nguyen

Fr. Adrian J. Sanchez

Fr. Justin S. Ramos

Fr. Luke S. Laslavich

Fr. Charles W. Willingham

Fr. Jordan S. Anderson

Fr. Gregory M. Dick

Fr. Nicholas M. Tacito

Fr. Augustine R. Puchner

Fr. Raphael J. Davis

Fr. Godfrey E. Bushmaker

Fr. Victor S. Szczurek

Fr. Alphonsus B. Hermes

Fr. Chrysostom A. Baer

Fr. John Henry E. Hanson

Fr. Andrew P. Tran

Fr. Sebastian A. Walshe

Fr. Damien V. Giap

Fr. Charbel R. Grbavac

Fr. Benedict M. Solomon

Fr. Ambrose G. Criste

Fr. Claude A. Williams

Rev. Frater Brendan R. Hankins

Frater Maximillian C. Okapal

Frater Alan V. Benander

Br. Mark R. Charlesworth

Frater David R. Gonzalez

Frater Nathaniel P. Drogin

Frater Stanislas L. Knuffke

Frater Cyprian W. Fritz
Frater Herman Joseph J. Putnam
Frater Jacob J. Hsieh
Frater Bruno D. Johnson
Frater Joachim A. Aldaba
Frater Vianney E. Ceja
Frater Miguel G. Batres
Frater Pio C. Vottola
Frater Clement R. Hurtgen
Frater Emmanuel Aldaba
Frater Basil Harnish
Frater Matthew Desmé
Frater Edmund Page
Frater Joshua Allen
Frater Simeon Goodwin

5. Now a death raised in the air which takes place on a tree, could be none other than the Cross: and again, in no other death are the hands and feet pierced, except on the Cross alone.

6. But since by the sojourn of the Savior among men–all nations also on every side began to know God; they did not leave this point, either, without a reference but mention is made of this matter as well in the Holy Scriptures. For "There shall come to pass in that day," he says, "the Root of Jesse Who shall arise to rule the nations, on Him the nations shall hope" (Isaiah 11:10). This then is a little in proof of what has happened.

7. But all Scripture teems with refutations of the disbelief of the Jews. For which of the righteous men and holy prophets, and patriarchs, recorded in the divine Scriptures, ever had his corporal birth of a virgin only? Or what woman has sufficed without man for the conception of human kind? Was not Abel born of Adam, Enoch of Jared, Noah of Lamech, and Abraham of Tera, Isaac of Abraham, Jacob of Isaac? Was not Judas born of Jacob, and Moses and Aaron of Amram? Was not Samuel born of Elkana, was not David of Jesse, was not Solomon of David, was not Hezekiah of Achaz, was not Josiah of Amos, was not Isaiah of Amos, was not Jeremiah of Hilkiah, was not Ezekiel of Buzi? Had not each a father as author of his existence? Who then is he that is born of a virgin only? For the prophet made exceeding much of this sign.

8. Or whose birth did a star in the skies forerun, to announce to the world him that was born? For when Moses was born, he was hid by his parents: David was not heard of, even by those of his neighborhood, inasmuch as even the great Samuel did not know him, but asked, if Jesse had yet another son. Abraham again became known to his neighbors as a great man only subsequently to his birth. But of Christ's birth the witness was not a man, but a star in that heaven from which He was descending.

✳

HORNS OF THE ALTAR

ST. CYRIL OF ALEXANDRIA[12]

T he horns of the altar [in the tabernacle] are somehow like hands which are spread out, and this prefiguring the shape of the honorable Cross...[And] the horns are four...because the altar is perfectly square, with all four sides of equal length, and its horns seem equal from all sides. And what is the reason of this? Because Christ, and Him crucified, is perceived in every place; and this is the glorious pride for those who believe in Him. Indeed, the divine Paul says, "But God forbid that I should boast except in the Cross of [our Lord Jesus] Christ, by Whom the world has been crucified to me, and I to the world" (Galatians 6:14)...

Accordingly, the divine Aaron went into the holy of holies once a year, through the blood of the purification for sins. Again, observe that Christ also is in this, with His own blood somehow sprinkled over His own Cross for the salvation and life of all. For the horns are a type of the Cross, spreading out this way and that, as in the order of His hands. Therefore, consider on the one hand, Christ dying once; and, on the other hand, being the Holy of holies, according to [His] nature, as God. For all creation, whether visible or invisible, is a partaker of Christ. And even the truthful John says "of His fullness we have all received" (John 1:16)...

Only notice that just as with the bull, Immanuel was slaughtered on our behalf, delivering us from sins, removing punishment, and entering "the greater and more perfect tabernacle" (Hebrews 9:11)–neither through [the blood] of bulls nor goats, but through His own blood and His death which He tasted of once and for all. Consider also that blood and water came out from His side on the Cross by means of the spear. As we have already said, the prominence of the horns is a type of the Cross.

---

[12] St. Cyril of Alexandria, *De Adoratione* 9.

❋

THE ARK OF THE CROSS

ST. JUSTIN MARTYR[13]

G od said in Isaiah to Jerusalem: "I saved you in the flood of Noah" (Isaiah 54:9). By this which God said was meant that the mystery of saved men appeared in the deluge. For righteous Noah, along with the other mortals at the deluge, i.e., with his own wife, his three sons and their wives, being eight in number, were a symbol of the eighth day, wherein Christ appeared when He rose from the dead, for ever the first in power. For Christ, being the First-born of every creature, became again the Chief of another race regenerated by Himself through water, and faith, and wood, containing the Mystery of the Cross; even as Noah was saved by wood when he rode over the waters with his household.

Accordingly, when the prophet says, "I saved you in the times of Noah," as I have already remarked, he addresses the people who are equally faithful to God, and possess the same signs. For when Moses had the rod in his hands, he led your nation through the sea. And you believe that this was spoken to your nation only, or to the land.

But the whole earth, as the Scripture says, was inundated, and the water rose in height fifteen cubits above all the mountains: so that it is evident this was not spoken to the land, but to the people who obeyed Him: for whom also He had before prepared a resting-place in Jerusalem, as was previously demonstrated by all the symbols of the deluge; I mean, that by water, faith, and wood, those who are afore-prepared, and who repent of the sins which they have committed, shall escape from the impending judgment of God.

---

[13] St. Justin the Martyr, *Dialogue with Trypho*, Chapter 138: "Noah is a Figure of Christ, Who Has Regenerated Us by Water, and Faith, and Wood (of the Cross)" ANF v. 1.

※

THE UNICORN'S HORNS

ST. JUSTIN MARTYR[14]

"Let Him be glorified among His brethren; His glory is that of the firstling of a bull; His horns the horns of a unicorn: on them shall He toss nations alike unto the very extremity of the earth" (Psalms 91:11).

N ow, no one could say or prove that the horns of a unicorn represent any other fact or figure than the type which portrays the Cross. For the one beam is placed upright, from which the highest extremity is raised up into a horn, when the other beam is fitted on to it, and the ends appear on both sides as horns joined on to the one horn. And the part which is fixed in the center, on which are suspended those who are crucified, also stands out like a horn; and it also looks like a horn conjoined and fixed with the other horns. And the expression, 'With these shall he push as with horns the nations from one end of the earth to another,' is indicative of what is now the fact among all the nations.

For some out of all the nations, through the power of this mystery, having been so pushed, that is, pricked in their hearts, have turned from vain idols and demons to serve God. But the same figure is revealed for the destruction and condemnation of the unbelievers; even as Amalek was defeated and Israel victorious when the people came out of Egypt, by means of the type of the stretching out of Moses' hands, and the name of Jesus, by which the son of Nun was called.[15] And it seems that the type and sign, which was erected to counteract the serpents which bit Israel, was intended for the salvation of those who believe that death was

---

[14] St. Justin the Martyr, *Dialogue With Trypho,* Chapter 91: "The Cross Was Foretold in the Blessings of Joseph, and in the Serpent that Was Lifted Up," ANF v. 1.

[15] That is, Joshua the Son of Nun.

declared to come thereafter on the serpent through Him that would be crucified, but salvation to those who had been bitten by him and had betaken themselves to Him that sent His Son into the world to be crucified. For the Spirit of prophecy by Moses did not teach us to believe in the serpent, since it shows us that he was cursed by God from the beginning [Genesis 3:14]; and in Isaiah [27:1] it tells us that he shall be put to death as an enemy by the mighty sword, which is Christ.

⁂

THE CROSS AND BAPTISM IN THE OLD TESTAMENT

EPISTLE OF BARNABAS[16]

L et us further inquire whether the Lord took any care to foreshadow the water [of Baptism] and the Cross. Concerning the water, indeed, it is written, in reference to the Israelites, that they should not receive that baptism which leads to the remission of sins, but should procure another for themselves. The prophet therefore declares, "Be astonished, O heaven, and let the earth tremble at this, because this people have committed two great evils: they have forsaken Me, a living fountain, and have hewn out for themselves broken cisterns. Is my holy hill Zion a desolate rock? For you shall be as the fledglings of a bird, which fly away when the nest is removed" (Isaiah 16:1, 2).

And again the prophet says, "I will go before you and make level the mountains, and will break the brazen gates, and bruise in pieces the iron bars; and I will give you the secret, hidden, invisible treasures, that they may know that I am the Lord God" (Isaiah

---

[16] *Epistle of Barnabas*, Chapter 11: "Baptism and the Cross Prefigured in the Old Testament," ANF v. 1

45:2,3). And "He shall dwell in a lofty cave of the strong rock" (Isaiah 33:16).

Furthermore, what does He say in reference to the Son? "His water is sure; you shall see the King in His glory, and your soul shall meditate on the fear of the Lord" (Isaiah 33:16-18).

And again He says in another prophet, "The man who does these things shall be like a tree planted by the courses of waters, which shall yield its fruit in due season; and his leaf shall not whither, and all that he does shall prosper. Not so are the ungodly, not so, but even as chaff, which the wind sweeps away from the face of the earth. Therefore the ungodly shall not stand in judgment, nor sinners in the counsel of the just; for the Lord knows the way of the righteous, but the way of the ungodly shall perish" (Psalms 1:3-6).

Realize how He has described at once both the water and the Cross. For these words imply that blessed are those who, placing their trust in the Cross, have gone down into the water. For, He says they shall receive their reward in due season [cf. Luke 12:42, Matthew 24:45] and then declares, "I will recompense them."

But now He says, "Their leaves shall not whither." This means that every word which proceeds out of your mouth in faith and love shall tend to bring conversion and hope to many.

Again, another prophet says, "And the land of Jacob shall be extolled above every land" (Zephaniah 3:19). This means the vessel of His Spirit, which He shall glorify. Furthermore, what does He say? "And there was a river flowing on the right, and from it arose beautiful trees; and whosoever shall eat of them shall live forever" (Ezekiel 47:12). This means that we indeed descend into the water full of sins and defilement, but come up, bearing fruit in our heart, having the fear [of God] and trust in Jesus in our spirit. "And whoever shall eat of these shall live for ever," This means: "Whoever," He declares, "shall hear you speaking, and believe, shall live forever."

✸

MOSES AND THE CROSS

EPISTLE OF BARNABAS[17]

I n like manner He points to the Cross of Christ in another prophet, who says, "And when shall these things be accomplished? And the Lord says, When a tree shall be bent down, and again arise, and when blood shall flow out of wood."[18]

Here again you have an intimation concerning the Cross, and Him Who would be crucified. Yet again He speaks of this in Moses, when Israel was attacked by strangers. And that He might remind them, when assailed, that it was on account of their sins they were delivered to death, the Spirit speaks to the heart of Moses, that he should make a figure of the Cross, and of Him about to suffer thereon; for unless they put their trust in Him [Psalm 2:12], they shall be overcome forever.

Moses therefore placed one weapon above another in the midst of the hill, and standing upon it, so as to be higher than all the people, he stretched forth his hands, and thus again Israel acquired the mastery. But when again he let down his hands, they were again destroyed. For what reason? That they might know that they could not be saved unless they put their trust in Him.

And in another prophet He declares, "All day long I have stretched forth My hands to an unbelieving people, and one that gainsays My righteous way" (Isaiah 65:2). And again Moses makes a type of Jesus, [signifying] that it was necessary for Him to suffer, [and also] that He would be the Author of life [to others], whom they believed to have destroyed on the cross when Israel was failing.

---

[17] *Epistle of Barnabas,* Chapter 12:"The Cross of Christ Frequently Announced in the Old Testament," ANF v. 1.

[18] Although it is no certain which citation this is from; some surmise Habakkuk 2:11.

For since transgression was committed by Eve through means of the serpent, [the Lord] brought it to pass that every [kind of] serpents bit them, and they died (cf. Numbers 21:6–9; John 3:14–18), that He might convince them, that on account of their transgression they were given over to the straits of death.

Moreover Moses, when he commanded that, "You shall not have any graven or molten [image] for your God" (Deuteronomy 27:15), did so that he might reveal a type of Jesus. Moses then makes a brazen serpent, and places it upon a beam, and by proclamation assembles the people. When, therefore, they were come together, they besought Moses that he would offer sacrifice in their behalf, and pray for their recovery. And Moses spoke unto them, saying, "When any one of you is bitten, let him come to the serpent placed on the pole; and let him hope and believe, that even though dead, it is able to give him life, and immediately he shall be restored" (Numbers 21:9). And they did so.

You have in this also [an indication of] the glory of Jesus; for in Him and to Him are all things (Colossians 1:16). What, again, does Moses say to Joshua the son of Nun, when he gave him this name, as being a prophet, with this view only, that all the people might hear that the Father would reveal all things concerning His Son Jesus to the son of Nave? This name then being given him when he sent him to spy out the land, he said, "Take a book into your hands, and write what the Lord declares, that the Son of God will in the last days cut off from the roots all the house of Amalek" (Exodus 17:14).

Behold again: Jesus who was manifested, both by type and in the flesh (cf. 1 Timothy 3:16), is not the Son of Man, but the Son of God. Since, therefore, they were to say that Christ was the son of David, fearing and understanding the error of the wicked, he says, "The Lord said unto my Lord, 'Sit at My right hand, until I make Your enemies Your footstool'" (Psalms 110:1; Matthew 22:43–45).

And again, thus Isaiah says, "The Lord said to Cyrus, my Anointed, whose right hand I have held, that the nations should yield obedience before Him; and I will break in pieces the strength of kings" (Isaiah 45:1). Behold how David called Him Lord and the Son of God.

※

THE BRAZEN SERPENT

ST. AUGUSTINE[19]

H e endured death, then; He hanged death on the Cross, and mortal men are delivered from death. The Lord calls to mind a great matter, which was done in a figure with them of old: "And as Moses," He says, "lifted up the serpent in the wilderness, so must the Son of man be lifted up; that every one who believes on Him may not perish, but have everlasting life" (John 3:14, 15).

A great mystery is here, as they who read know. Again, let them hear, as well they who have not read as they who have forgotten what perhaps they had heard or read. The people Israel were fallen helplessly in the wilderness by the bite of serpents; they suffered a great calamity by many deaths: for it was the stroke of God correcting and scourging them that He might instruct them.

In this was shown a great mystery, the figure of a thing to come: the Lord Himself testifies in this passage, so that no man can give another interpretation than that which the truth indicates concerning itself.

Now Moses was ordered by the Lord to make a brazen serpent, and to raise it on a pole in the wilderness, and to admonish the people Israel, that, when any had been bitten by a serpent, he should look to that serpent raised up on the pole. This was done: men were bitten; they looked and were healed.

What are the biting serpents? Sins, from the mortality of the flesh.

---

[19] St. Augustine, *Tractates on John*, 12.11, NPNF s. 1, v. 7.

What is the serpent lifted up? The Lord's death on the cross. For as death came by the serpent, it was figured by the image of a serpent. The serpent's bite was deadly, the Lord's death is life-giving.

A serpent is gazed on that the serpent may have no power. What is this? A death is gazed on, that death may have no power.

But whose death? The death of life: if it may be said, the death of life; indeed, for it may be said, but said wonderfully. But should it not be spoken, seeing it was a thing to be done? Shall I hesitate to utter that which the Lord has condescended to do for me?

Is not Christ the Life? And yet Christ hung on the Cross. Is not Christ Life? And yet Christ was dead. But in Christ's death, death died. Life dead slew death; the fullness of life swallowed up death; death was absorbed in the Body of Christ. So also shall we say in the resurrection, when now triumphant we shall sing, "Where, O death, is your contest? Where, O death, is your sting?" (cf. 1 Corinthians 15:55).

Meanwhile brethren, that we may be healed from sin, let us now gaze on Christ crucified; for "as Moses," says He, "lifted up the serpent in the wilderness, so must the Son of man be lifted up; that whosoever believes on Him may not perish, but have everlasting life." Just as those who looked on that serpent perished not by the serpent's bites, so those who look in faith on Christ's death are healed from the bites of sins. But those were healed from death to temporal life; while here He says, "that they may have everlasting life."

Now there is this difference between the figurative image and the real thing: the figure procured temporal life; the reality, of which that was the figure, procures eternal life.

✣

CARRYING THE CROSS

✳

CARRY YOUR CROSS

ST. CYRIL OF ALEXANDRIA[1]

T hose who are skilled in combat are pleased by the acclaim of the spectators, urged on by the hope of rewards to the victory of their calling. However, those who aspire to divine rewards and thirst for a share in that which is laid up for the blessed, gladly face the contests which are endured for love of Christ.

They live blameless lives, not clinging to sloth, which merits no reward; neither do they yield to unworthy cowardice, but bear themselves bravely against all temptation, making light of the attacks of their persecutors; believing that to suffer for the Lord is great gain. For they are mindful of what the blessed Paul has said, "That the sufferings of this time are not worthy to be compared with the glory to come, that should be revealed in us" (Romans 8:18).

So behold the all-beautiful disposition of things our Lord Jesus Christ now arranges for the profit and edification of His holy apostles. For He says to them: "If anyone desires to come after me, let him deny himself, take up his cross, and follow Me. For whoever desires to save his life will lose it; but he who loses his life for My sake shall find it" (Matthew 16:24, 25).

This precept is a salutary one, worthy of the sanctified; one which leads to heavenly glory and conducting us to a joyful destiny. For the will to suffer for Christ will not go unrewarded. No, but more surely, it will bring us the joy of eternal life and glory. But it was to be expected that the disciples who were not yet endowed with the power from on high (Luke 24:49) would succumb to human foolishness and thinking within themselves,

---

[1] St. Cyril of Alexandria, Sermon Given at Ephesus in the Church dedicated to St. Mary, *Homily 9*, PG 77.1009.

would say, "How can anyone deny himself? How can one who has lost his life find it again? What comparable reward can be given to those who have suffered this loss? And also, in what kind of reward will he share?

In order to remove such thoughts and words from their minds–and also to change them and uplift them to largeness of soul, awaking within them a desire for the glory He will bestow on them–He says: "I say to you there are some standing here who shall not taste death until they see the Son of Man coming in His kingdom" (Matthew 16:28).

Does this mean that their lifetime would be lengthened so that they could reach those days at the end of the ages, in which He will come down from heaven and restore to the saints the kingdom that was prepared for them? He surely could do this as well, for He can do all things (Psalms 57:2); and there is nothing which cannot be done by His almighty command. He calls His kingdom this vision of His glory in which he shall presently be seen; and in which He shall shine before them as the sun upon the earth. For He shall come in the glory of God the Father, not in the lowliness that belongs to us.

※

AN ANCIENT PRACTICE

ST. BASIL THE GREAT[2]

The doctrines and proclamations (*kerygmata*) that are preserved in the Church are given to us in two different ways: the doctrines are given to us in written teachings, and the proclamations have been given to us secretly, through the apostolic tradition...to start with the first and the most common among

---

2 St. Basil the Great, *On the Holy Spirit*, 27, 188.

them, whoever has ever taught us in writing the sign of the Cross, which signifies our hope in our Lord Jesus Christ?

⁂

THE POWER OF THE CROSS

ST. ATHANASIUS THE APOSTOLIC[3]

S ince [St. Antony] did not permit his acquaintances to enter [his cave], they often used to spend days and nights outside, and heard as it were crowds inside [his cave] shouting, clamoring, and sending forth pitiful voices and crying, "Go from what is ours. What are you even doing in the desert? You cannot endure our attack."

So at first those outside thought there were some men fighting with him, and that they had entered by ladders; but when stooping down they saw through a hole there was nobody, they were afraid, accounting them to be demons, and they called on Antony.

Them he quickly heard, though he had not given a thought to the demons, and coming to the door he besought them to depart and not to be afraid, 'For thus,' said he, 'the demons make their seeming onslaughts against those who are cowardly. Sign yourselves therefore with the Cross, and depart boldly, and let these make sport for themselves.'

So they departed fortified with the sign of the Cross. But he remained in no way harmed by the evil spirits, nor was he wearied with the contest, for there came to his aid visions from above, and the weakness of the foe relieved him of much trouble and armed him with greater zeal. For his acquaintances used often to come expecting to find him dead, and would hear him chanting:

"'Let God arise and let all His enemies be scattered, let those also who hate Him flee from before His face. As smoke vanishes,

---

[3] St. Athanasius the Apostolic, *Life of Antony*, 13.

let them vanish; as wax melts before the face of fire, so let the sinners perish from the face of God" (Psalms 67:1, 2). And again, "All nations surrounded me, but in the Name of the Lord I will destroy them" (Psalms 117:11).

⚹

SOLDIERS CRUCIFIED TO THE WORLD

ST. JOHN CHRYSOSTOM[4]

L et no man be ashamed of the honored symbols of our salvation, and of the greatest of all good things, whereby we even live, and whereby we are; but as a crown, so let us bear about the Cross of Christ. Yes, for by it all things are wrought, that are wrought among us. Whether one is newborn, the Cross is there; or to be nourished with that Mystical Food, or to be ordained, or to do anything else, everywhere our symbol of victory is present. Therefore both on house, walls, and windows; and upon our forehead and our mind, we inscribe it with much care.

For of the salvation wrought for us, and of our common freedom, and of the goodness of our Lord, this is the sign. "For as a sheep was He led to the slaughter"(Isaiah 53:7). Therefore, when you sign yourself, think of the purpose of the Cross, and quench anger, and all the other passions. When you sign yourself, fill your forehead with all courage, make your soul free, and know assuredly what are the things that give freedom. Therefore, also Paul leading us there, I mean unto the freedom that befits us, did on this wise lead us unto it, having reminded us of the cross and blood of our Lord. "For you are bought," he says, "at a price; do not be slaves of men" (1 Corinthians 7:23). Consider, how he says, the price that has been paid for you, and you will be a slave to no man; by the price meaning the Cross.

---

[4] St. John Chrysostom, *Commentary on the Gospel According to St. Matthew*, Homily 56.7, 8, NPNF s. 1, v. 10.

Since not merely by the fingers ought one to engrave it, but before this by the purpose of the heart with much faith. And if in this way you have marked it on your face, none of the unclean spirits will be able to stand near you, seeing the blade whereby he received his wound, seeing the sword which gave him his mortal stroke. For if we, on seeing the places in which the criminals are beheaded, shudder; think what the devil must endure, seeing the weapon, whereby Christ put an end to all his power, and cut off the head of the dragon.

So, do not be ashamed of so great a blessing, lest Christ be ashamed of you, when He comes with His glory, and the sign appears before Him, shining beyond the very sunbeam. For indeed the Cross comes then, uttering a voice by its appearance, and pleading with the whole world for our Lord, and signifying that no part has failed of what pertained to Him.

This sign, both in the days of our forefathers and now, has opened doors that were shut; this has quenched poisonous drugs; this has taken away the power of hemlock[5]; this has healed bites of venomous beasts. For if it opened the gates of hell, and threw wide the archways of Heaven, and made a new entrance into Paradise, and cut away the nerves of the Devil; what marvel, if it prevailed over poisonous drugs, and venomous beasts, and all other such things.

Therefore, engrave this upon your mind, and embrace the salvation of our souls. For this Cross saved and converted the world, drove away error, brought back truth, made earth Heaven, fashioned men into angels. Because of this, the devils are no longer terrible, but contemptible; neither is death, death, but a sleep. Because of this, all who war against us is cast to the ground, and trodden under foot.

If anyone therefore says to you, "Do you worship the crucified?" Say, with your voice full of all joy, and your countenance gladdened, "I do both worship Him, and will never cease to

---

[5] Hemlock is a highly poisonous plant with a spoiled stem.

worship." And if he laughs, weep for him, because he is mad. Thank the Lord, that He has bestowed on us such benefits, as one cannot so much as learn without His revelation from above. Why, this is the very reason of his laughing, that "the natural man does not receive the things of the Spirit" (1 Corinthians 2:14).

Since our children also feel this, when they see any of the great and marvelous things; and if you bring a child into the mysteries, he will laugh. Now the heathen are like these children; or rather they are more imperfect even than these; wherefore also they are more wretched, in that not in an immature age, but when full grown, they have the feelings of babes; wherefore neither are they worthy of indulgence.

But let us with a clear voice, shouting both loud and high, cry out and say (and should all the heathen be present, so much the more confidently), that "The Cross is our glory, 'the sum of all our blessings, our confidence, and all our crown." I wish that with Paul I were also able to say, "By whom the world is crucified to me, and I to the world" (Galatians 6:14), but I cannot, restrained as I am by various passions.

Therefore, I admonish both you, and surely before you, myself, to be crucified to the world, and to have nothing in common with the earth, but to set your love on your country above, and the glory and the good things that come from it. For indeed we are soldiers of a heavenly King, and are clad with spiritual arms. Why then take we upon ourselves the life of traders, and mountebanks, no rather of worms? For where the King is, there should also the soldier be. Yea, we are become soldiers, not of them that are far off, but of them that are near. For the earthly king indeed would not endure that all should be in the royal courts, and at his own side, but the King of the Heavens desires all to be near His royal throne.

And how, one may say, is it possible for us, being here, to stand by that throne? Because Paul too being on earth was where the seraphim, where the cherubim are; and nearer to Christ, than these the bodyguards to the king. For these turn about their faces in many directions, but him nothing beguiled nor distracted, but he kept his whole mind intent upon the king. So that if we would, this is possible to us also.

For were He distant from us in place, you might well doubt, but if He is present everywhere, to him that strives and is in earnest He is near. Wherefore also the prophet said, "I will fear no evil, for You are with me" (Psalms 22:4). God Himself said again, "I am a God Who is near at hand, and not afar off" (Jeremiah 23:23). Then as our sins separate us from Him, so does our righteousness draw us nigh unto Him. "For while you are still speaking," it is said, "I will say, 'Here I am'" (Isaiah 58:9).

What father would ever be this obedient to his offspring? What mother is there, so ready, and continually standing, if haply her children call her? There is not one, no father, no mother: but God stands continually waiting, if any of his servants should perhaps call Him; and never, when we have called as we should, has He refused to hear. Therefore He says, "While you are still speaking," I do not wait for you to finish, and I will immediately hear.

Therefore, let us call Him as it is His will to be called. But what is this, His will? "Loose," he says, "every bond of iniquity, untie the knots of violent dealings, set the bruised free, and cancel every unjust contract Break your bread for the hungry, and lead the unsheltered poor to your house; if you see one naked, clothe him, and you shall not disregard your seed in your own house. Then shall your light break forth as the morning, and your health shall speedily spring forth; and your righteousness shall go before you, and the glory of God shall surround you. Then shall you cry, and God will hear you; while you are yet speaking He will say, 'Behold, here I am'" (Isaiah 58:6-10).

And we may ask, who is able to do all this? No, who is unable, I ask you? For which is difficult of the things I have mentioned? Which is laborious? Which not easy?

Why, they are not only so entirely possible only, but even easy, that many have actually overshot the measure of those sayings, not only tearing in pieces unjust contracts, but even stripping themselves of all their goods; making the poor welcome not to roof and table, but even to the sweat of their body, and laboring in order to maintain them; doing good not to kinsmen only, but even to enemies.

But what is there at all even hard in these sayings? For neither did He say, "Pass over the mountain, go across the sea, dig through so many acres of land, abide without food, wrap yourself in sackcloth," but, "Impart to the poor...impart of your bread...cancel every unjust contract."

What is more easy than this? Tell me.

Even if you account it difficult, look, I pray you, at the rewards also, and it shall be easy to you. For much as our emperors at the horse races heap together before the combatants crowns, and prizes, and garments, even so Christ also sets His rewards in the midst of His course, holding them out by the prophet's words, as it were by many hands. The emperors, although they may be even ten thousand emperors, yet as being men, and the wealth which they have in a course of spending, and their munificence of exhaustion, are ambitious of making the little appear much; wherefore also they commit each thing severally into the hand of the several attendants, and so bring it forward. But our King contrariwise, having heaped all together (because He is very rich, and does nothing for display), He so brings it forward, and what He so reaches out is indefinitely great, and will need many hands to hold it. And to make you aware of this, examine each particular of it carefully.

"Then," He says, "shall your light break forth as the morning." Does not this gift appear to you as someone thing? But it is not one; no, for it has many things in it, both prizes, and crowns, and other rewards. And, if you are minded, let us take it to pieces and show all its wealth, as it shall be possible for us to show it; only do not you grow weary.

And first, let us learn the meaning of "It shall break forth." For He said not at all, "shall appear," but "shall break forth," declaring to us its quickness and plentifulness, and how exceedingly He desires our salvation, and how the good things themselves travail to come forth, and press on; and that which would check their unspeakable force shall be nought; by all which He indicates their plentifulness, and the infinity of His abundance.

But what is "the morning"? It means, "not after being in life's temptations, neither after our evils have come upon us"; no, it is quite beforehand with them. For as in our fruits, we call that early, which has shown itself before its season; so also here again, declaring its rapidity, he has spoken in this way, much as above He said, "While you are still speaking, I will say, Behold, here I am."

But of what manner of light is He speaking, and what can this light be? Not this, that is sensible; but another far better, which shows us Heaven, the angels, the archangels, the cherubim, the seraphim, the thrones, the dominions, the principalities, the powers, the whole host, the royal palaces, the tabernacles.

For if you should be counted worthy of this light, you will both see these, and be delivered from hell, and from the venomous worm, and from the gnashing of teeth, and from the bonds that cannot be broken, and from the anguish and the affliction, from the darkness that has no light, and from being cut asunder, and from the river of fire, and from the curse, and from the abodes of sorrow; and you shalt depart, "where sorrow and grief have fled away" (Isaiah 35:10); where great is the joy, and the peace, and the love, and the pleasure, and the mirth; where is life eternal, and unspeakable glory, and inexpressible beauty; where are eternal tabernacles, and the untold glory of the King, and those good things, "which eye has not seen, nor ear heard, neither have entered into the heart of man" (1 Corinthians 2:9); where is the spiritual bridal chamber, and the apartments of the heavens, and the virgins that bear the bright lamps, and they who have the marriage garment; where many are the possessions of our Lord, and the storehouses of the King.

See how great the rewards, and how many He has set forth by one expression, and how He brought all together?! So also by unfolding each of the expressions that follow, we shall find our abundance great, and the ocean immense. Shall we then still delay, I beg you; and be backward to show mercy on them that are in need?

No, I entreat, but though we must throw away all, be cast into the fire, venture against the sword, leap upon daggers, suffer what you will; let us bear all easily, that we may obtain the garment of the kingdom of Heaven, and that untold glory; which may we all attain, by the grace and love towards man of our Lord Jesus Christ, to Whom be glory and might, unto the age of ages. Amen.

�֎

MY ONLY BOAST

ST. JOHN CHRYSOSTOM[6]

"But God forbid that I should boast except in the Cross of our Lord Jesus Christ..." (Galatians 6:14)

Truly this symbol is thought despicable; but it is so in the world's reckoning, and among men; in Heaven and among the faithful it is the highest glory. Poverty too is despicable, but it is our boast; and to be cheaply thought of by the public is a matter of laughter to them, but we are elated by it. So too is the Cross our boast. He does not say, "I boast not," nor, "I will not boast," but, "Far be it from me that I should," as if he abominated it as absurd, and invoked the aid of God to his success therein.

And what is the boast of the Cross? That Christ for my sake took on Him the form of a slave, and bore His sufferings for me the slave, the enemy, the unfeeling one; yea He so loved me as to give Himself up to a curse for me. What can be comparable to this! If servants who only receive praise from their masters, to whom they are akin by nature, are elated thereby, how must we not boast when the Master who is very God is not ashamed of the

---

[6] St. John Chrysostom, *Commentary on Galatians* 6:14, NPNF s. 1, v. 13.

Cross which was endured for us. Let us then not be ashamed of His unspeakable tenderness; He was not ashamed of being crucified for thy sake, and wilt thou be ashamed to confess His infinite solicitude? It is as if a prisoner who had not been ashamed of his King, should, after that King had come to the prison and himself loosed the chains, become ashamed of him on that account. Yet this would be the height of madness, for this very fact would be an especial ground for boasting.

"...through which the world has been crucified to me, and I to the world" (Galatians 6:15).

What he here calls the world is not the heaven nor the earth, but the affairs of life, the praise of men, retinues, glory, wealth, and all such things as have a show of splendor. To me these things are dead. Such a one it behooves a Christian to be, and always to use this language. Nor was he content with the former putting to death, but added another, saying, "and I unto the world," thus implying a double putting to death, and saying, They are dead to me, and I to them, neither can they captivate and overcome me, for they are dead once for all, nor can I desire them, for I too am dead to them. Nothing can be more blessed than this putting to death, for it is the foundation of the blessed life.

✳

WITNESS TO THE CROSS

ST. POLYCARP OF SMYRNA[7]

For whosoever does not confess that Jesus Christ has come in the flesh, is antichrist" (1 John 4:3).

---

[7] St. Polycarp of Smyrna, *Epistle to the Philippians*, Chapter 7: "Avoid the Docetae, and Persevere in Fasting and Prayer," ANF v. 1.

A nd whosoever does not confess the witness[8] of the Cross is of the Devil; and whosoever perverts the oracles of the Lord to his own lusts, and says that there is neither a resurrection nor a judgment, he is the first-born of Satan.[9] Wherefore, forsaking the vanity of many, and their false doctrines, let us return to the word which has been handed down to us from the beginning; "keep watch and pray" (1 Peter 4:7), and persevering in fasting; beseeching in our supplications the all-seeing God "lead us not into temptation" (Matthew 6:13, 26:41) as the Lord has said: "The spirit truly is willing, but the flesh is weak" (Matthew 26:41; Mark 14:38).

※

ACCEPTING INSULTS AND DEATH

ST. JOHN CHRYSOSTOM[10]

L ong-suffering is a marvelous thing. It places the soul as in a quiet harbor, freeing it from tossings and evil spirit. And Christ has taught us this everywhere, but especially now, when He is judged and dragged, and led about...

But why was it that Pilate did not make the inquiry in their presence, but apart, having gone into the judgement hall? He suspected something great regarding Him...Concerning that of which Pilate must have desired to hear, namely His Kingdom. For He answered, "My Kingdom is not of this world" (John 18:36). That is, "I am indeed a King, yet not such a one as you suspect, but far more glorious"...

---

[8] Literally, "martyrdom."

[9] Probably the original is contained in Eusebius, *Church History*, 4.14. It became a commonplace expression in the Church.

[10] St. John Chrysostom, *Homilies on John*, 84.1-3, 85.1-3, NPNF v. 1, s. 14, pp. 313, 314, 317-319.

But they cried out, "We have no king but Caesar." Of their own will they subjected themselves to punishment. Therefore, God also gave them up because they were the first to cast themselves out from His providence and superintendence...

And why did they strive to kill Him in this manner? It was a shameful death. Fearing, therefore, lest there should afterward be any remembrance of Him, they desired to bring Him to the accursed punishment, not knowing that truth is exalted by hindrances...

The crown of thorns, the robe, the reed, the blows, the smiting on the cheek, the spittings, the irony—these things, if continually meditated on are sufficient to take down all anger. And if we are mocked at, if we suffer injustice, let us still say, "The servant is not greater than his Master" (John 13:16)...For on one account He bore all these things, so that we might walk in His footsteps and endure those mocking which disturb more than any other kind of reproach...

This let us also imitate; for nothing so much makes God so gracious as loving enemies, and doing good to those who despitefully use us. When a man insults you, do not look to him, but to the devil who moves him. Against him, empty all your wrath; but pity the man who is moved by him. For if lying is from the devil, to be angry without a cause is much more so...

He went forth bearing the Cross as a trophy over the tyranny of death: and as conquerors do, He bore upon the shoulders the symbol of victory...

They crucified Him with thieves, in this also unintentionally fulfilling prophesy, since the Prophet had foretold of old, that "He was numbered with the transgressors" (Isaiah 53:12)...Three were crucified, but Jesus alone was glorious so that you may learn that His power affected all...

But no one attributed anything of what was done to either of the others, but only to Jesus; so entirely was the plot of the devil rendered vain...For even of these two, one was saved. Therefore, he did not insult the glory of the Cross, but contributed to it not a little...And Pilate wrote a title...At the same time, requiting the Jews and making a defense for Christ...Pilate thus placed, as on a trophy those letters which utter a clear voice and show forth His victory and proclaim His Kingdom, though not in its completeness. And this he made manifest not in a single tongue, but in three languages...in order that none might be ignorant of the defense, he publicly recorded the madness of the Jews in all the languages. For they bore malice against Him even when crucified.

But He, on the Cross, committed His mother to the disciple, teaching us even to our last breath to show every care for our parents...Here He shows much loving affection...It was no little thing for [St. John] to be honored with such honor and to receive the reward of steadfastness...He did everything without being troubled, speaking with the disciple concerning His mother, fulfilling prophesies, holding forth good hopes to the thief...

Let us not tremble at death. Our soul has by nature the love of life, but it lies with us either to loose the bands of nature and make this desire weak, or else to tighten them and make the desire more tyrannous...

But why did He make no mention of any other woman, although another stood there? To teach us to pay more than ordinary respect to our mothers. For as when parents oppose us on spiritual matters, we must not even own them, so when they do not hinder us, we should pay them all becoming respect...

He was everywhere wanting to show that this Death was of a new kind, if indeed the whole lay in the power of the Person dying, and death did not come on the Body before He willed it; and he willed it after He had fulfilled all things...Do you see how strong is truth? By means of the very things which are the objects of their zeal, prophesy is fulfilled...

For the soldiers when they came broke the legs of the others, but not those of Christ. Yet to gratify the Jews they pierced His side with a spear and now insulted the dead Body...[for] there was a prophesy saying, "They shall look on Him Whom they pierced" (Zechariah 12:10), and "A bone of Him shall not be broken" (Numbers 9:12; Exodus 12:46).

With this also an ineffable mystery was accomplished. For "There came forth water and blood." Those founts come forth for no reason, but because the Church consists of these two together. And the Initiated know it, being regenerated by water and nourished by the Blood and the Flesh. From this the Mysteries take their beginning. So when you approach that awesome cup, you may also approach as drinking from the very Side.

❋

NAILED TO THE CROSS

ST. IGNATIUS OF ANTIOCH [11]

I glorify the God and Father of our Lord Jesus Christ, Who by Him has given you such wisdom. For I have observed that you are perfected in an immoveable faith, as if you were nailed to the Cross of our Lord Jesus Christ, both in the flesh and in the spirit, and are established in love through the blood of Christ, being fully persuaded, in very truth, with respect to our Lord Jesus Christ, that He was the Son of God, "the Origin of every creature," God the Word, the Only-Begotten Son, and was of the seed of David according to the flesh, by the Virgin Mary; was baptized by John, that all righteousness might be fulfilled by Him (Matthew 3:15); that He lived a life of holiness without sin, and was truly, under Pontius Pilate and Herod the tetrarch, nailed [to the Cross] for us in His flesh. From Whom we also derive our being, from His divinely-blessed passion, that He might set up a standard for the ages (cf. Isaiah 5:26, 49:22), through His Resurrection, to all His holy and faithful [followers], whether among Jews or Gentiles, in the one body of His Church.

---

[11] St. Ignatius, *Epistle to the Smyrnaeans*, Chapter 1: "Thanks to God for Your Faith," ANF v. 1.

❋

SIFT ME AS WHEAT

ST. IGNATIUS OF ANTIOCH [12]

I die for Christ of my own choice, unless you hinder me. I beseech you not to show inopportune kindness to me. Let me be given to the wild beasts, for by their means I can attain to God. I am God's wheat, and I am being ground by the teeth of the beasts so that I may appear as pure bread. I rather coax the beasts, that they may become my tomb, and leave no part of my body behind, that I may not be a nuisance to anyone when I have fallen asleep. Then I will truly be a disciple of Jesus Christ, when the world shall not even see my body. Entreat the Lord for me that through these instruments I may appear as a sacrifice to God. I do not lay injunctions on you, as Peter and Paul did. They were Apostles; I am a convict. They were free; I am a slave, up till now: but if I suffer, then am I a freed man of Jesus Christ, and shall rise free in him. Now I am learning in my bonds to abandon all desire.

5. From Syria to Rome I am fighting with wild beasts, by land and sea, by night and by day, being bound among ten leopards, I mean the squad of soldiers, who become worse in return for their gratuities. But through the wrongs they do me I become more of a disciple, "yet I am not justified on this account" (1 Corinthians 4:4). I hope I may have profit of the wild beasts that have been got ready for me: and I pray that they may prove expeditious with me: and I will coax them to eat me up expeditiously, and not refuse to touch me through cowardice, as they have done in some cases. Why, if they refuse though I am willing, I will force them to it. I ask your indulgence; I know what is for my good; now I am beginning to be a disciple: may nothing, of things visible and invisible, grudge my attaining to Jesus Christ. Let all come, fire and cross and conflicts with beasts, hacking, cutting, wrenching of

---

[12] St. Ignatius, *Epistle to the Romans*, 4-7, ANF v. 1.

bones, chopping of limbs, the crushing of my body, cruel chastisements of the devil laid upon me. Only let me attain to Jesus Christ.

6. My birth pangs are at hand. Bear with me, my brothers. Do not hinder me from living. Do not wish for my death. Do not make the world a present of one who wishes to be God's. Do not coax him with material things. Allow me to receive the pure light; when I arrive there I shall be a real man. Permit me to be an imitator of the Passion of my God...

7. I write to you while alive, yet longing for death; my desire has been crucified and there is not in me any sensuous fire, but living water bounding up in me, and saying inside me, "Come to the Father." I have no pleasure in food which is destined for corruption, nor in the delights of this life. I desire the Bread of God, which is the Flesh of Christ Who was of the seed of David; and for drink I desire His Blood which is incorruptible love.

※

MOTHERS AND THE CROSS

ST. JEROME[13]

M others, wean your children, love them, but pray for them that they may long live above this earth, not on the earth but above it, for there is nothing long-lived on this earth, and that which lasts long is but short and very frail. Warn them rather to take up the Cross of the Lord than to love this life.

109. Mary, the mother of the Lord stood by her Son's Cross; no one has taught me this but the holy Evangelist St. John. Others have related how the earth was shaken at the Lord's passion, the sky was covered with darkness, the sun withdrew itself; that the thief was after a faithful confession received into paradise. John

---

[13] St. Jerome, *Epistle 63*, §§108-111, NPNF, s. 2, v. 10

tells us what the others have not told, how the Lord fixed on the Cross called to His mother, esteeming it of more worth that, victorious over His sufferings, He rendered her the offices of piety, than that lie gave her a heavenly kingdom. For if it be according to religion to grant pardon to the thief, it is a mark of much greater piety that a mother is honored with such affection by her Son. "Behold," He says, "your Son" and "Behold your mother" (John 19:26, 27).

Christ testified from the Cross, and divided the offices of piety between the mother and the disciple. The Lord made not only a public but also a private testament, and John signed this testament of His, a witness worthy of so great a Testator. A good testament not of money but of eternal life, which was written not with ink but with the Spirit of the living God, Who says: "My tongue is the pen of a quickly writing scribe" (Psalms 45:1).

110. Nor was Mary below what was becoming the mother of Christ. When the apostles fled, she stood at the Cross, and with pious eyes beheld her Son's wounds, for she did not look for the death of her Offspring, but the salvation of the world. Or perhaps, because that "royal hall" knew that the redemption of the world would be through the death of her Son, she thought that by her death also she might add something to the public weal. But Jesus did not need a helper for the redemption of all, Who saved all without a helper. Therefore also He says: "I am become like a man without help, free among the dead." He received indeed the affection of His mother, but sought not another's help.

111. Imitate her, holy mothers, who in her only dearly beloved Son set forth so great an example of maternal virtue; for neither have you sweeter children, nor did the Virgin seek the consolation of being able to bear another son.

112. Masters, command your servants not as being below you in rank, but as remembering that they are sharers of the same nature as yourselves. Servants, serve your masters with good will, for each ought patiently to support that to which he is born, and be obedient not only to good but also to froward masters. For what

thanks has your service if you zealously serve good masters? But if you thus serve the obstinate also you gain merit; for the free also have no reward, if when they transgress they are punished by the judges, but this is their merit to suffer without transgressing. And so you, if contemplating the Lord Jesus you serve even difficult masters with patience, will have your reward. Since the Lord Himself suffered, the just at the hand of the unjust, and by His wonderful patience nailed our sins to His Cross, that he who shall imitate Him may wash away his sins in His Blood.

113. In fine, turn all to the Lord Jesus. Let your enjoyment of this life be with a good conscience, your endurance of death with the hope of immortality, your assurance of the resurrection through the grace of Christ; let truth be with simplicity, faith with confidence, abstinence with holiness, industry with soberness, conversation with modesty, learning without vanity; let there be soberness of doctrine, faith without the intoxication of heresy.

The grace of our Lord Jesus Christ be with you all. Amen.

§ ✚ ҫ

THE GLORY OF THE CROSS

St. Cyril of Jerusalem[1]

---

[1] From *Catechetical Lecture 13* attributed to him in NPNF s. 2, v. 7.

The Cross is the Greatest Glory

Every deed of Christ is a cause of glorying to the Catholic Church, but her greatest of all glorying is in the Cross; and knowing this, Paul says, "But God forbid that I should boast except in the Cross of Christ" (Galatians 6:14). For wondrous indeed it was, that one who was blind from his birth should receive sight in Siloam;² but what is this compared with the blind of the whole world? A great thing it was, and passing nature, for Lazarus to rise again on the fourth day; but the grace extended to him alone, and what was it compared with the dead in sins throughout the world? Marvelous it was, that five loaves should pour forth food for the five thousand; but what is that to those who are famishing in ignorance through all the world? It was marvelous that she should have been loosed who had been bound by Satan eighteen years: yet what is this to all of us, who were fast bound in the chains of our sins?

But the glory of the Cross led those who were blind through ignorance into light, loosed all who were held fast by sin, and ransomed the whole world of mankind.

The Saving Power of the Cross

Do not be surprised that the whole world was released; for it was no mere man, but the Only-Begotten Son of God, Who died on its behalf. Moreover one man's sin, even Adam's, had power to bring death to the world; but "if by the trespass of the one death reigned over the world," how shall not life much rather "reign by the righteousness of the One" (Romans 5:17, 18)? And if because of the tree of food they were then cast out of paradise, shall not believers now more easily enter into paradise because of the Tree of Jesus? If the first man formed out of the earth brought in universal death, shall not He who formed him out of the earth bring in eternal life, being Himself the Life? If Phineas, when he waxed zealous and slew the evildoer, staved the wrath of God, shall not

---

² Cf. St. Athanasius, *de Incarnatione*, 18, 49.

Jesus, who slew not another, but "gave up Himself for a ransom" (1 Timothy 2:6), put away the wrath which is against mankind?

He was Sinless

Let us then not be ashamed of the Cross of our Savior, but rather glory in it. For the word of the Cross is to Jews a stumbling-block, and unto Gentiles foolishness, but to us salvation: and to those who are perishing it is foolishness, but "to us who are being saved it is the power of God (cf. 1 Corinthians 1:18, 23). For it was not a mere man who died for us, as I said before, but the Son of God, God made man. Further; if the lamb under Moses drove the destroyer (cf. Exodus 12:23) far away, did not much rather "the Lamb of God, Who takes away the sin of the world" (John 1:29), deliver us from our sins?

[For, if] the blood of a senseless sheep could promise salvation; would not the Blood of the Only-Begotten much rather save? If anyone disbelieves the power of the Crucified, let him ask the devils; if anyone does not believe words, let him believe what he sees. Many have been crucified throughout the world, but by none of these are the devils scared. But when they see even the Sign of the Cross of Christ, Who was crucified for us, they shudder.[3]

For those men died for their own sins, but Christ for the sins of others; for He "committed no sin, neither was guile found in His mouth" (1 Peter 2:22; from Isaiah 53:9). It is not Peter who says this, for then we might suspect that he was partial to his Teacher; but it is Isaiah who says it, who was not indeed present with Him in the flesh, but in the Spirit foresaw His coming in the flesh.

Yet why now bring the prophet only as a witness? Take for a witness Pilate himself, who gave sentence upon Him, saying, "I find no fault with this Man" (Luke 23:14): and when he gave Him up, and had washed his hands, he said, "I am innocent of the blood of this just Person" (Matthew 27:24). There is yet another witness

---

[3] See also *Catechetical Lectures* 1.3; 17.35, 36.

of the sinlessness of Jesus: the robber, the first man admitted into Paradise who rebuked his fellow, and said, "We receive the due reward of our deeds; but this man has done nothing wrong (Luke 23:41)...for we were present, both you and I, at His judgment."[4]

His Suffering Was True and Real

Jesus then really suffered for all men; for the Cross was no illusion, otherwise our redemption is an illusion also. His death was not a mere show, for then is our salvation also mythical. If His death was but a show, they were true who said, "We remember that that deceiver said, while He was yet alive, 'After three days I rise again'" (Matthew 27:63).

His Passion, then, was real: for He was really crucified, and we are not ashamed of this; He was crucified, and we do not deny it. Not at all. Rather, I glory to speak of it. For though I should now deny it, here is Golgotha to refute me, near which we are now assembled; the Wood of the Cross refutes me, which was afterwards distributed over time from here to all the world.[5]

I confess the Cross, because I know of the Resurrection. For if, after being crucified, He had remained as He was, I would not have confessed it, for I might have concealed both it and my Master; but now that the Resurrection has followed the Cross, I am not ashamed to declare it.

The Cross Was Not a Punishment

Being then in the flesh like others, He was crucified, but not for the like sins. For He was not led to death for covetousness, since He was a Teacher of poverty; nor was He condemned for lust, for He Himself says plainly, "Whosoever looks at a woman to

---

[4] Cf. *Catechetical Lectures* 13.30, 31. The Benedictine Editor remarks, "We know not whence Cyril took the notion that the two robbers were present at the trial of Jesus." Perhaps this may be inferred from the sentence of crucifixion was pronounced on them at the same time as on Jesus.

[5] Cf. *Catechetical Lectures* 4.10; 10.19; and Chapter Four, above.

lust for her has already committed adultery with her" (Matthew 5:28); not for smiting or striking hastily, for He turned the other cheek also to the stutter: not for despising the Law, for He was the fulfiller of the Law; not for reviling a prophet, for it was Himself who was proclaimed by the prophets; not for defrauding any of their hire, for He ministered without reward and freely; not for sinning in words, or deeds, or thoughts, He Who "did no sin, neither was guile found in His mouth; who when He was reviled, reviled not again; when He suffered, threatened not" (1 Peter 2:22, 23); Who came to His passion, not unwillingly, but willing. And even you dissuade Him now, saying, "Far be it from You, Lord," He will say again, "Get behind Me, Satan!" (Matthew 16:22, 23).

How Christ Willingly Accepted the Cross as a Great Glory

And will you be persuaded that He came to His passion willingly? Others, who do not know in advance, die unwillingly. But He spoke before of His passion, "the Son of Man will be delivered up to be crucified" (Matthew 26:2). But do you know why this Friend of man did not avoid death? It was so that the whole world should not perish in its sins. "Behold, we are going up to Jerusalem, and the Son of Man will be betrayed...and crucified" (Matthew 20:18); and again, "He steadfastly set His face to go to Jerusalem" (Luke 9:51).

And do you certainly know that the Cross is a glory to Jesus? Hear His own words, not mine. Judas had become ungrateful to the Master of the house, and was about to betray Him. Having but just now gone forth from the table, and drunk His cup of blessing, in return for that drought of salvation he sought to shed righteous blood.

"My own familiar friend...ate My bread, lifted up his heel against Me" (Psalms 419, NKJV); his hands were but lately receiving the blessed gifts,[6] and presently for the wages of betrayal he was plotting His death. And being reproved, and having heard that word, "You have said it" (Matthew 26:25), he again went out. Then said Jesus, "The hour is coming that the Son of Man should be glorified" (John 12:23).

Do you see how He knew the Cross to be His proper glory? For if Isaiah is not ashamed of being sawn asunder, should Christ be ashamed of dying for the world? Now the Son of man is glorified. Not that He was without glory before: for He was "glorified with the glory" (John 13:31) which was before "the foundation of the world" (John 17:5). He was ever glorified as God; but now He was to be glorified in wearing the Crown of His patience.

He did not give up His life by compulsion, nor was He put to death by murderous violence, but of His own accord. Hear what He says: "I have power to lay down My life, and I have power to take it again" (John 10:18). I yield it of My own choice to My enemies; for unless I chose, this could not be. He came therefore of His own set purpose to His passion, rejoicing in His noble deed, smiling at the crown, cheered by the salvation of mankind; not ashamed of the Cross, for it was to save the world. For it was no common man who suffered, but God in man's nature, striving for the prize of His patience.

---

[6] That is, the "eulogia" which Judas partook of and not the Holy Body and Precious Blood. The meaning of this was clarified also by St. John Chrysostom and St. Cyril of Alexandria, which is referred to in the church today as the blessed bread distributed to the faithful, apart from the Holy Body, Life-Giving Bread, or Eucharistic Bread. It also was customary in the first few centuries to bless the eulogia and distribute them to others who did not partake of the Holy Communion during the Divine Liturgy. This was later forbidden from being sent into foreign dioceses, which may have been used for other purposes (See Synod of Laodicea, Canon 14; and Hefele's comments, Councils, vol. 2, p. 308; Eusebius, Ecclesiastical History, 5.24).

The Rejection of the Jews

But the Jews contradict this[7] since they are always ready to object, and backward to believe. For this reason the prophet just now read says, "Lord, who has believed our report?" (Isaiah 53:1). For the Persians believe (cf. Acts 2:9), and Hebrews do not believe; they shall see, to whom He was not spoken of, and "those who have not heard shall understand" (Romans 15:21, quoting Isaiah 52:1) while they who study these things shall set at naught what they study. They speak against us, and say, "Does the Lord then suffer? What? Did men's hands have power over His sovereignty?"

Read the Lamentations; for in those Lamentations, Jeremiah, lamenting you, wrote what is worthy of lamentations. He saw your destruction, he beheld your downfall, he bewailed Jerusalem which then was; for that which now is shall not be bewailed; for that Jerusalem crucified the Christ (cf. Galatians 5:24), but that which now is worships Him. Lamenting then he says, The breath of our countenance, Christ the Lord was taken in our corruptions. Am I then stating views of my own? Behold he testifies of the Lord Christ seized by men. And what is to follow from this? Tell me, O prophet.

He says, "The breath of our nostrils, the anointed of the Lord, was taken in their pits, of Whom we said, 'Under His shadow we shall live among the nations'" (Lamentations 4:20). For he signifies that the grace of life is no longer to dwell in Israel, but among the Gentiles.

The Prophesies Point to the Cross

But since there has been much opposition by them, come, let me, with the help of your prayers (as the shortness of the time may allow) set forth by the grace of the Lord some few testimonies

---

[7] There is so close a resemblance between the remainder of this Lecture and the explanation of the same article of the Creed by Rufinus, that the Byzantine editor states: "I have no doubt that Rufinus drew from Cyril's fountains." Cf. Rufinus, *de Symbolo*, §19, sqq.

concerning the Passion. For the things concerning Christ are all put into writing, and nothing is doubtful, for nothing is without a text. All are inscribed on the monuments of the prophets; clearly written, not on tablets of stone, but by the Holy Spirit.

Since then you have heard the Gospel speaking concerning Judas, should you now receive the testimony to it? You have heard that He was pierced in the side by a spear; shouldn't you also see where this is written? You have heard that He was crucified in a garden; shouldn't you also see where this is written? You have heard that He was sold for thirty pieces of silver; shouldn't you learn what prophet said this? You have heard that He was given vinegar to drink; learn where this also is written. You have heard that His body was laid in a tomb, and that a stone was set over it; shouldn't you receive this testimony also from the prophet? You have heard that He was crucified with robbers; shouldn't you also see where this is written? You have heard that He was buried; shouldn't you see whether the circumstances of His burial are anywhere accurately written? You have heard that He rose again; shouldn't you see whether we mock you in teaching these things? "For my speech and my preaching were not with persuasive words of human wisdom" (1 Corinthians 2:4).[8]

We stir now no sophistical contrivances; for these become exposed; we do not conquer words with words. For these come to an end; "but we preach Christ Crucified" (1 Corinthians 1:23), Who has already been preached previously by the prophets.

But do you, I ask, receive the testimonies, and seal them in your heart. And, since they are many, and the rest of our time is narrowed into a short space, listen now to a few of the more important as time permits; and having received these beginnings, be diligent and seek out the remainder. "Let not your hand be only

---

[8] The simple style of the New Testament is also defended by the Scholar Origen, *Against Celsus*, 3.68, among others. St. Cyril alludes to the same proverb in the *Homily on the Paralytic*, c. 14: "Word resists word, but a deed is irresistible."

stretched out to receive, but let it be also ready to work."⁹ God gives all things freely. "For if any of you lacks wisdom, let him ask of God who gives" (James 1:5), and he shall receive. May He through your prayer grant utterance to us who speak, and faith to you who hear.

The Prophesies Concerning the Betrayal of Judas

Let us then seek the testimonies to the Passion of Christ: for we are met together, not now to make a speculative exposition of the Scriptures, but rather to be certified of the things which we already believe. Now you have received from me first the testimonies concerning the coming of Jesus; and concerning His walking on the sea, for it is written, "Your way is in the sea" (Psalms 76:20).

Also, concerning diverse cures you have on another occasion received testimony. Now therefore I begin from whence the Passion began. Judas was the traitor, and he came against Him, and stood, speaking words of peace, but plotting war. Concerning him, therefore, the Psalmist says, "My friends and My neighbors drew near against Me, and stood" (Psalms 37:12). And again, "Their words were smoother than oil, yet they are spears" (Psalms 54:22). "Greetings, Master" (Matthew 26:49); yet he was betraying his Master to death. He was not ashamed by His warning, when He said, "Judas, do you betray the Son of Man with a kiss?" (Luke 22:48). For what He said to him was just this, "Recollect your own name; Judas means confession"¹⁰; you have covenanted, you have received the money, make confession quickly.

---

⁹ "Do not let your hand be stretched out to receive, and shut when you should repay" (Sirach 4:31). This verse is quoted in the *Didache*, 4; *Epistle of Barnabas*, 19; and *Apostolic Constitutions*, 7.11.

¹⁰ Philo writes: "And his name was called Judah, which being interpreted is "confession to the Lord" (*Jud. de Plantatione Noë*, 33). In Genesis 49:8 the name is differently interpreted: "Judah, you are he whom your brethren shall praise." The root has both senses "to confess," and "to praise," which are closely allied since to "confess" is to "give God the glory" (Joshua 7:19).

"O God, pass not over My praise in silence; for the mouth of the sinner, and the mouth of the deceitful, are opened against Me; they have spoken against Me with a treacherous tongue, they have compassed Me about also with words of hatred" (Psalms 108:1-3).

But that some of the chief priests also were present, and that He was put in bonds before the gates of the city, you have heard before, if you remember the exposition of the Psalm, which has told the time and the place; how they returned at evening, and hungered like dogs, and encompassed the city (cf. Psalms 58:7).[11]

The Thirty Pieces of Silver

Listen also about the thirty pieces of silver. And I will say to them, "If it is good in your sight, give me my price, or refuse" (Zechariah 11:12), and the rest. One price is owing to Me from you for My healing the blind and lame, and I receive another; for thanksgiving, dishonor, and for worship, insult.

See how the Scripture foresaw these things? "And they weighed for My price thirty pieces of silver" (Zechariah 11:12). How exact the prophecy! How great and unerring the wisdom of the Holy Spirit! For he said, not ten, nor twenty, but thirty, exactly as many as there were. Tell also what becomes of this price, O Prophet! Does he who received it keep it? Or does he give it back? And after he has given it back, what becomes of it?

The Prophet says then, "And I took the thirty pieces of silver, and cast them into the house of the Lord, into the smelting furnace" (Zechariah 11:13). Compare the Gospel with the Prophecy: "Judas," it says, "was remorseful…and cast down the pieces of silver in the temple, and departed" (Matthew 27:3, 5).

The Potter's House

But now I have to seek the exact solution of this seeming discrepancy. For those who make light of the prophets, allege that

---

[11] The exposition was probably given in a sermon preached to the whole congregation, although not in these Lectures.

the prophet says on the one hand, "And I cast them into the house of the Lord," into the workshop, but the Gospel on the other hand, "And they gave them for the potter's field" (Matthew 27:3, 7).

Hear then how they are both true. Indeed, those conscientious Jews, the High Priests of that time, when they saw that Judas repented and said, "I have sinned, in that I have betrayed innocent blood," replied, "What is that to us, you see to it" (Matthew 27:4). Is it then nothing to you, the crucifiers? But shall he who received and restored the price of murder see to it, and shall you the murderers not see to it? Then they say among themselves, "It is not lawful to cast them into the treasury, because it is the price of blood" (Matthew 27:6).

Out of your own mouths is your condemnation; if the price is polluted, the deed is polluted also. But if you are fulfilling righteousness in crucifying Christ, why don't you receive the price of it? The point of inquiry is this: how is there no disagreement, if the gospel says, the potter's field (Matthew 27:7,10), and the prophet (Zechariah 11:12, 13), the workshop? No, but not only people who are goldsmiths, or brass-founders, have a workshop, but potters also have workshops for their clay. For they sift off the fine and rich and useful earth from the gravel, and separate from it the mass of the refuse matter, and temper the clay first with water, that they may work it with ease into the forms intended. Why then do you wonder that the Gospel says plainly the potter's field, whereas the prophet spoke his prophecy like an enigma, since prophecy is in many places enigmatical?

The Prophesies Concerning the Evil Counsel Against Him

They bound Jesus, and brought Him into the hall of the High Priest. And so you would learn and know that this also is written, Isaiah says, "Woe unto their soul, for they have taken evil counsel against themselves, saying, 'Let us hand over the Just One, for He is troublesome to us'" (Isaiah 3:9, 10).[12] And truly, woe unto their soul! Let us see how.

Isaiah was sawn asunder, yet after this the people was restored. Jeremiah was cast into the mire of the cistern, yet was the wound of the Jews healed; for the sin was less, since it was against man. But when the Jews sinned, not against man, but against God in man's nature, "Woe unto their soul!–Let us bind the Just."

Could He not then set Himself free, someone will say; He, who freed Lazarus from the bonds of death on the fourth day, and loosed Peter from the iron bands of a prison? Angels stood ready at hand, saying, "Let us break their bonds in pieces" (Psalms 2:3); but they are held back, because their Lord willed to undergo it. Again, He was led to the Judgment Seat before the elders; you have already the testimony to this: "The Lord Himself will enter into judgment with the ancients of His people, and with the princes thereof" (Isaiah 3:14).

The Prophesies of the Scourge and Blows

But the High Priest having questioned Him, and heard the truth, is cruel; and the wicked officer of wicked men smites Him; and the countenance, which had "shone as the sun" (Matthew 17:2), endured to be smitten by lawless hands. Others also come and spit on the face of Him, who by spittle had healed the man who was blind from his birth.

"Is this how you repay the Lord? O foolish and unwise people" (Deuteronomy 32:6). And the prophet greatly wondering, says, "Lord, who has believed our report?" (Isaiah 53:1). For the thing is incredible, that God, the Son of God, and "the Arm of the Lord" (Isaiah 53:1) should suffer such things.

But in order that those who are being saved may not disbelieve, the Holy Spirit writes before, in the person of Christ,

---

[12] In the Septuagint, from which St. Cyril quotes, there is an evident interpolation of Wisdom 2:12: "Let us lie in wait for the righteous; because he is not for our turn."

who says–for He Who then spoke these things, was afterward Himself an actor in them–"I gave My back to the scourges" (Isaiah 50:6), "for Pilate, when he had scourged Him, delivered Him to be crucified" (Matthew 27:26); and "My cheeks to blows; and My face I turned not away from the shame of spitting" (Isaiah 50:6), saying, as it were: "Though I know before that they will smite Me, I did not even turn My cheek aside; for how should I have nerved My disciples against death for truth's sake, had I Myself dreaded this? For I said, 'He who loves his life shall lose it' (John 12:25). If I had loved My life, how was I to teach without practicing what I taught?"

First then, being Himself God, He endured to suffer these things at the hands of men; that after this, we men, when we suffer such things at the hands of men for His sake, might not be ashamed. Realize that of these things also the prophets have clearly written beforehand. Many, however, of the Scripture testimonies I pass by for want of time, as I said before; for if one should exactly search out all, not one of the things concerning Christ would be left without witness.

He Was Presented Before Rulers

Having been bound, He came from Caiaphas to Pilate. Is this also written? Yes; "And having bound Him, they led Him away as a present to the king of Jarim" (Hosea 10:6).[13] But here some sharp hearer will object, "Pilate was not a king" (to leave for a while the main parts of the question), "how then having bound Him, led they Him as a present to the king?" But read the gospel: "When

---

13 Alternatively, "It also shall be carried unto Assyria for a present to King Jareb." This passage is applied in the same manner to Luke 23:7 by St. Justin the Martyr, *Dialogue with Trypho*, §103); the Scholar Tertullian, *Against Marcion*, 4.42; and Rufinus, *de Symbolo*, §21, who adds,–"And rightly does the Prophet add the name 'Jarim,' which means 'a wild vine,' for Herod was...a wild vine, i.e. of an alien stock." For the various interpretations of the name see the Commentaries on Hosea 5:13 and 10:6, see Cuneijorm Schrader, *Inscriptions*, II. §439; Driver, *Introduction to Old Testament Literature*, p. 283.

Pilate heard that He was of Galilee, he sent Him to Herod (Luke 23:6, 7); for Herod was then king, and was present at Jerusalem. And now observe the exactness of the Prophet; for he says, that He was sent as a present; "for the same day Pilate and Herod were made friends together, for before they were at enmity" (Luke 23:12). For it became Him who was on the eve of making peace between earth and heaven, to make the very men who condemned Him the first to be at peace; for the Lord Himself was there present, Who "reconciles the hearts of the princes of the earth" (cf. Job 12:24). Mark the exactness of the prophets, and their true testimony.

They Wrongly Judged the Judge of the World

So, look with awe at the Lord who was judged. He allowed Himself to be led and carried by soldiers. Pilate sat in judgment, and He who sits on the right hand of the Father, stood and was judged. The people whom He had redeemed from the land of Egypt, and oftentimes from other places, shouted against Him, "Away with Him, away with Him! Crucify Him!" (John 19:15).

Why, O Jews? Because He healed your blind? Or because He made your lame to walk, and bestowed His other benefits? So that the Prophet in amazement speaks of this too, "Against whom have you opened your mouth, and against whom have you let loose your tongue?" (Isaiah 57:4). And the Lord Himself says in the Prophets, "My inheritance became to Me as a lion in the forest; it raised its voice against Me; therefore have I hated it...I have not refused them, but they have refused Me; in consequence thereof I say, I have forsaken My house" (Jeremiah 12:8, 7).

He Held His Peace

When He was judged, He held His peace; so that Pilate was moved for Him, and said, "Do You not hear how many things they testify against You?" (Matthew 27:13). Not that he knew Him Who was judged, but he feared his own wife's dream which had been reported to him. And Jesus held His peace. The Psalmist says, "And I became as a man who does not hear; and in whose mouth are no reproofs" (Psalms 37:14); and again, "But I was as a deaf man and heard not; and as a dumb man that opened not his mouth" (Psalms 37:13). You have already heard about this [in another homily], if you remember.

Even Their Mocking Shows He is a King

But the soldiers who crowd around mock Him, and their Lord becomes a sport to them, and upon their Master they make jests. "When they looked at Me, they wagged their heads" (Psalms 108:25). Yet the figure of kingly state appears; for though in mockery, yet they bend the knee. And the soldiers before they crucify Him, put on Him a purple robe, and set a crown on His head; for what though it be of thorns? Every king is proclaimed by soldiers; and Jesus also must in a figure be crowned by soldiers; so that for this cause the Scripture says in the Canticles, "Go forth, O you daughters of Jerusalem, and look upon King Solomon in the crown with which His mother crowned Him" (Song of Songs 3:11). And the crown itself was a mystery; for it was a remission of sins, a release from the curse.

He Assumes Adam's Curses and Turns Them Into Blessings

Adam received the sentence, "Cursed is the ground in your labors; thorns and thistles shall it bring forth in your labors" (Genesis 3:17, 18).[14] For this cause Jesus assumes the thorns, that He may cancel the sentence; for this cause also was He buried in the earth, that the earth which had been cursed might receive the blessing instead of a curse. At the time of the sin, they clothed themselves with fig-leaves; for this cause Jesus also made the fig-tree the last of His signs. For when about to go to His passion, He curses the fig-tree, not every fig-tree, but that one

---

[14] The Septuagint differs from other readings in one Hebrew letter, rendering "in your labors" instead of "for your sake."

alone, for the sake of the figure; saying, "No more let any man eat fruit from you" (Mark 11:14); let the doom be cancelled.

And because they previously clothed themselves with fig-leaves, He came at a season when food was not usually found on the fig-tree. Who does not know that in winter the fig-tree bears no fruit, but is clothed with leaves only? Was Jesus ignorant of this, which all knew? No, but although He knew, yet He came as if seeking; not ignorant that He should not find, but showing that the emblematical curse extended to the leaves only.

The Types of the Garden of Eden and the Sacrificial Lamb

And since we have touched on things connected with Paradise, I am truly astonished at the truth of the types. In Paradise was the Fall, and in a Garden was our Salvation.

From the Tree came sin, and until the Tree sin lasted. In the evening, when the Lord walked in the Garden, they hid themselves (Genesis 3:8.); and in the evening the robber is brought by the Lord into Paradise. But someone will say to me, "You are inventing subtleties; show me from some prophet the Wood of the Cross; unless you give me a testimony from a prophet, I will not be persuaded."

Hear then from Jeremiah, and assure yourself; "I was like a harmless lamb led to be slaughter; did I not know it?" (Jeremiah 11:19).[15] For read it as a question, in the way that I have read it. For didn't He know, Who said, "You know that after two days comes the Passover, and the Son of Man will be delivered up to be crucified" (Matthew 26:2). Then, how could he not know? So, "I was like a harmless lamb led to be slaughtered; did I not know it?"

---

[15] The extant translations of this text make the text complicate its interpretation. "I was like a gentle lamb led to the slaughter; and I did not know that they had devised devices against me" (NKJV); "I was like a gentle lamb led to the slaughter; and I did not know that they devised schemes/plots against me" (*NRSV, NAS*); "I did not know I was like an innocent lamb led to be sacrificed" (*Orthodox Study Bible*). The author here inserts an interrogative.

But what kind of lamb? Let John the Baptist interpret it, when he says, "Behold the Lamb of God, Who carries away the sin of the world" (John 1:29). "They devised against Me a wicked device, saying" (Jeremiah 11:19). Doesn't He who knows the devices also know the result of them? And what did they say: "Come, and let us place wood in His bread" (Jeremiah 11:19).[16]

And if the Lord deems you worthy, you shall later learn, that His body according to the Gospel bore the figure of bread. "Come then, and let us place a beam upon His bread, and cut Him off out of the land of the living." Life is not cut off, why do you labor for nothing? "Let His Name be blessed unto the ages; His Name shall remain before the sun" (Psalms 71:17)[17] abides in the Church.

And that it was Life, which hung on the Cross, Moses says, weeping, "And your life shall hang before your eyes; and you shall be afraid day and night, and you shall not trust your life" (Deuteronomy 28:66). And so too, what was just now read as the text, "Lord, who has believed our report?" (Isaiah 53:1).

The Brazen Serpent

This was the figure which Moses completed by fixing the serpent to a cross, that "whoever had been bitten by the living serpent, and looked to the brazen serpent, might be saved by

---

[16] This LXX reading also finds other variants: "Let us destroy the tree with its fruit" (*NKJV, NAS, NRSV*), in which "fruit" is proverbially rendered from the literal word, "bread." This interpretation of the Cross is also used by St. Justin the Martyr, *Dialogue with Trypho*, 72; in which he accuses the Jews of having recently cut out the passage because of the supposed reference to Christ. The Scholar Tertullian also writes: "Of course on His body that 'wood' was put; for so Christ has revealed, calling His body 'bread'" (*Against the Jews*, c. 10; see also *Against the Marcionites*, 3.19; 55.40). These early explanations are continued in the writings of St. Cyprian (*Testimonia ad Quirinum*, Lib. 2.15) and St. Athanasius (*De Incarnatione*, §33)).

[17] Although the LXX reading fits the context, the translator's text gives a distinct meaning: "And His name shall be remembered no more. Vain is your counsel; for before the sun His Name"

believing" (Numbers 21:9; John 2:14).[18] Does then the brazen serpent save when crucified, and shall not the Son of God incarnate save when crucified also? On each occasion life comes by means of wood.

For in the time of Noah the preservation of life was by an ark of wood. In the time of Moses the sea, on beholding the emblematical rod, was abashed at him who smote it; is then Moses' rod mighty, and is the Cross of the Savior powerless? But I pass by the greater part of the types, to keep within measure. The wood in Moses' case sweetened the water (cf. Exodus 15:25); and from the side of Jesus the water flowed upon the wood (cf. John 19:34).

Various Interpretations of the Blood and Water

The beginning of signs under Moses was blood and water; and the last of all Jesus' signs was the same. First, Moses changed the river into blood (Exodus 7:20); and Jesus at the last gave forth from His side water with blood.

(1) This was perhaps on account of the two speeches, his who judged Him, and theirs who cried out against Him; or because of the believers and the unbelievers. For Pilate said, "I am innocent...and he took water and washed his hands...and the people cried out and said, 'His blood be upon us'" (Matthew 27:24, 25): there came therefore these two out of His side; the water, perhaps, for him who judged Him; but for them that shouted against Him the blood.

(2) And again it is to be understood in another way; the blood for the Jews, and the water for the Christians: for upon them as plotters came the condemnation from the blood but to you who

---

[18] The Jerusalem editor asks, "How did Moses complete the figure by fixing the serpent to a cross? First he set up the wood and fixed it in the earth as a post: then by putting the brazen serpent across it he formed a figure of the Cross." cf. *Epistle of Barnabas*, 12; St. Justin the Martyr, *Apology*, 1.60; St. Irenaeus, *Hoeos*, 4.2; the Scholar Tertullian, *Against the Jews*, 10.

now believe, the salvation which is by water. For nothing has been done without a meaning.

(3) Our fathers[19] who have written comments have given another reason of this matter. For since in the gospels the power of salutary baptism is twofold, one which is granted by means of water to the illuminated, and a second to holy martyrs, in persecutions, through their own blood, there came out of that saving Side blood and water (John 19:34; cf. Song of Songs 3:10), to confirm the grace of the confession made for Christ, whether in baptism, or on occasions of martyrdom.

(4) There is another reason also for mentioning the Side. The woman, who was formed from the side, led the way to sin; but Jesus who came to bestow the grace of pardon on men and women alike, was pierced in the side for women, that He might undo the sin.

The Cross is a Crown, not a Dishonor

And whoever will inquire, will find other reasons also; but what has been said is enough, because of the shortness of the time, and that the attention of my hearers may not become full. However, we never can be tired of hearing concerning the crowning of our Lord, and least of all in this most holy Golgotha. For others only hear, but we both see and handle. Let none be weary; take your armor against the adversaries in the cause of the Cross itself; set up the faith of the Cross as a trophy against the gainsayers. For when you are going to dispute with unbelievers concerning the Cross of Christ, first make with your hand the sign of Christ's Cross, and the gainsayer will be silenced. Do not be

---

[19] The Scholar Origen gives two readings of this as well. First, "It is the Baptism of blood alone that can render us purer than the Baptism of water has done" (*Lib. Judic. Hom.* 7.2). He also writes: "If Baptism promises remission of sins, as we have received concerning Baptism in water and the Spirit, and if one who has endured the Baptism of Martyrdom receives remission of sins, then with good reason martyrdom may be called a baptism" (*Commentary on the Gospel of Matthew*, 16.6).

ashamed to confess the Cross; for angels glory in it, saying, "We know Whom you seek, Jesus the Crucified" (Matthew 28:5). You might not say, O angel, "I know whom you seek, my Master?" But, "I," he says with boldness, "I know the Crucified." For the Cross is a Crown, not a dishonor.

Take the Cross in Times of Persecution and Times of Peace

Now let us return to the proof from the Prophets which I spoke of. The Lord was crucified; you have received the testimonies. Do you see this spot of Golgotha? You answer with a shout of praise, as if assenting. See that you recant not in time of persecution!

Rejoice not in the Cross in time of peace only, but hold fast the same faith in time of persecution also; be not in time of peace a friend of Jesus, and His foe in time of wars. You receive now remission of your sins, and the gifts of the King's spiritual bounty; when war shall come, strive nobly for your King.

Jesus, the Sinless, was crucified for you; and will you not be crucified for Him who was crucified for you? You are not bestowing a favor, for you have first received; but you are returning a favor, repaying your debt to Him who was crucified for you in Golgotha.

Now Golgotha is interpreted, "the place of a skull." Who were they then, who prophetically named this spot Golgotha, in which Christ the true Head endured the Cross? As the apostle says, "Who is the Image of the Invisible God" and a little after, "and He is the Head of the body, the Church" (Colossians 1:15, 18). And again, "The Head of every man is Christ" (1 Corinthians 11:3).And again, "Who is the Head of all principality and power" (Colossians 2:10). The Head suffered in "the place of the skull."

O wondrous prophetic appellation! The very name also reminds you, saying, "Do not think of the Crucified as a mere man; He is the Head of all principality and power. That Head which was crucified is the Head of all power, and has for His Head the Father; for 'the Head of the man is Christ, and the Head of Christ is God'(1 Corinthians 11:3)."

The Darkness Prophesied

Christ then was crucified for us, Who was judged in the night, when it was cold, and therefore a fire of coals (John 18:18) was laid. He was crucified at the third hour;[20] and from the sixth hour there was darkness until the ninth hour (Matthew 27:45); but from the ninth hour there was light again. Are these things also written? Let us inquire.

Now the prophet Zechariah says, "And it shall come to pass in that day, that there shall not be light, and there shall be cold and frost one day (the cold on account of which Peter warmed himself); and that day shall be known to the Lord" (Zechariah 14:6, 7). What, did He not know the other days? There are many days, but "this is the day of the Lord's patience, which the Lord made" (Psalms 107:24). And that day shall be known unto the Lord, not day, and not night what is this dark saying which the Prophet speaks?

That day is neither day nor night. Then what shall we name it? The gospel interprets it, by relating the event. It was not day; for the sun shone not uniformly from his rising to his setting, but from the sixth hour till the ninth hour, there was darkness at midday. The darkness therefore was interposed; but "God called the darkness night" (Genesis 1:5). Therefore it was neither day nor night: for neither was it all light, that it should be called day; nor was it all darkness, that it should be called night; but after the ninth hour the sun shone forth.

This also the prophet foretells; for after saying, "not day, nor night," he added, "And at evening time it shall be light" (Zechariah

---

[20] That is, the hour in which the sufferings began, although He was nailed to the wood of the Cross in the sixth hour.

14:7).[21] Do you see the exactness of the prophets? Do you see the truth of the things which were written previously?

The Exact Hour of Darkness Prophesied

But, you may ask, what is the exact hour that the sun failed? Was it the fifth hour, or the eighth, or the tenth? Tell, O Prophet, this exact time to the Jews, who are unwilling to hear; when shall the sun go down? The prophet Amos answers, "And it shall come to pass in that day, says the Lord God, that the sun shall go down at noon (for there was darkness from the sixth hour) and the light shall grow dark over the earth in the day" (Amos 8:9).[22] What sort of season is this, O Prophet, and what sort of day?

"And I will turn your feasts into mourning; for this was done in the days of unleavened bread, and at the feast of the Passover." Afterwards he says, "And I will make Him as the mourning of an Only Son, and those with Him as a day of anguish" (Amos 8:10). For in the day of unleavened bread, and at the feast, their women were wailing and weeping, and the Apostles had hidden themselves and were in anguish. Wonderful then is this prophecy.

His Robe and Tunic

But, someone will say, "Give me yet another sign; what other exact sign is there of that which has come to pass? Jesus was crucified; and He wore but one robe, and one cloak: now His cloak the soldiers shared among themselves, having rent it into four; but His robe was not rent, for when rent it would have been no longer of any use; so about this lots are cast by the soldiers; thus the one they divide, but for the other they cast lots. Is then this also written?

---

[21] "It was not day, because of the noontide darkness: and again it was not night, because of the day which followed upon it which he represented by a song in saying, at evening time there shall be light" Eusebius, *Dem. Evang.* 10.7.

[22] Cf. Eusebius, *Dem. Evang.* 10.6.

They know, the diligent chanters[23] of the Church, who imitate the angelic hosts, and continually sing praises to God: who are thought worthy to chant Psalms in this Golgotha, and to say, "They divided My garments among them, and for My clothing they cast lots" (Psalms 21:19; John 19:24). The "lots" were what the soldiers cast.

The Scarlet Robe

Again, when He had been judged before Pilate, He was clothed in red; for there they put on Him a purple robe. Is this also written? Isaiah says, "Who is this that comes from Edom? The redness of His garments is from Bosor" (Isaiah 63:1, 2). Who is this who wears purple in dishonor? For Bosor has some such meaning in Hebrew.[24]

"Why are Your garments red, and Your raiment as from a trodden winepress?" But He answers and says, "All day long have I stretched forth My hands to a disobedient and contradictory people" (Isaiah 65:2).[25]

His Outstretched Hands

He stretched out His hands on the Cross, that He might embrace the ends of the world; for this Golgotha is the very center of the earth. It is not my word, but it is a prophet who has said,

---

[23] Cf. Synod of Laodicea, Canon 16.15: "Besides the appointed singers, who mount the ambo and sing from the book, others shall not sing in the Church." Hefele thinks that this was not intended to forbid the laity to take any part in the Church hymns, but only to forbid those who were not chanters to take the lead. See Rev. Joseph Bingham, *Antiquities of the Christian Church*, 3.7, 14.1; London: Oxford, 1840.

[24] *Bosor* or *Bozrah* means a "sheepfold," the capital of Edom (Genesis 36:33; 1 Chronicles 1:44; Isaiah 34:6; 63:1; Jeremiah 49:13; Amos 1:12).

[25] From the first centuries, the Fathers of the Church saw the Cross prefigured in Isaiah 65:2. Cf. *Epistle of Barnabas*, 12; Didache, 16; St. Justin the Martyr, *Apology*, 1.35; *Dialogue with Trypho*, 97, 114; Tertullian, *Against the Jews*, 12; St. Irenaeus, *Fragments from Lost Writings*, 55, 33.12, ANF v. 1.

"You have wrought salvation in the midst of the earth" (Psalms 73:12). The passage does not refer to Palestine especially: "in the midst of the earth" is equivalent to "in the sight of all nations."

He stretched forth human hands, who by His spiritual hands had established the heaven; and they were fastened with nails, that His manhood, which here the sins of men, having been nailed to the tree, and having died, sin might die with it, and we might rise again in righteousness. For since by one man came death, by One Man came also life (cf. Romans 5:12, 17); by One Man, the Savior, dying of His own accord: for remember what He said, "I have power to lay down My life, and I have power to take it again" (John 10:18).

"I thirst"

But though He endured these things, having come for the salvation of all, yet the people returned Him an evil recompense. Jesus said, "I thirst" (John 19:28). He who had brought forth the waters for them out of the uneven rock; and He asked fruit of the vine which He had planted.

But what is this vine? This vine, which was by nature of the holy fathers, but of Sodom by purpose of heart, "for their vine is of Sodom, and their fields of Gomorrah" (Deuteronomy 32:32). This vine, when the Lord thirsted, having filled a sponge and put it on a reed, offers Him vinegar. "They gave Me also gall for My food, and in My thirst, they gave Me vinegar to drink" (Psalms 68:22).

Do you see the clearness of the prophets' description? But what sort of gall did they put into His mouth? "They gave Him," it says, "wine mingled with myrrh" (Mark 15:23). Now myrrh is in taste like gall, and very bitter. Are these things what you repay the Lord? Are these your offerings, O vine, unto your Master?

Rightly did the Prophet Isaiah previously bewail you, saying, "My well-beloved had a vineyard in a hill in a fruitful place; and (not to recite the whole) I waited, He says, that it should bring forth grapes; I thirsted that it should give wine; but it brought forth thorns" (Isaiah 5:1, 2). So see the crown with which I am adorned. What then shall I now decree? "I will command the clouds that they rain no rain upon it" (Isaiah 5:6).[26]

For the clouds which are the prophets were removed from them, and are for the future in the Church; as Paul says, "Let the prophets speak two or three, and let the others judge" (1 Corinthians 14:29); and again, "God gave in the Church, some, apostles, and some, prophets" (Ephesians 4:11). Agabus, who bound his own feet and hands, was a prophet (cf. Acts 21:10, 11).

The Two Thieves

Concerning the robbers who were crucified with Him, it is written, "And He was numbered with the transgressors" (Isaiah 53:12). Both of them were before this transgressors, but one was so no longer. For the one was a transgressor to the end, stubborn against salvation; who, though his hands were fastened, smote with blasphemy by his tongue. When the Jews passing by wagged their heads, mocking the Crucified, and fulfilling what was written, "When they looked at Me, they wagged their heads" (Psalms 108:25). He also reviled with them. But the other rebuked the reviler; and it was to him the end of life and the beginning of restoration; the surrender of his soul a first share in salvation.

And after rebuking the other, he says, "Lord, remember me" (Luke 23:40 ff.), for with You is my account. Pay no attention to this man, for the eyes of his understanding are blinded; but "Remember me." I do not say, "Remember my works," for concerning these I am afraid. Every man has a feeling for his fellow-traveller; I am traveling with You towards death. So, remember me, Your fellow-wayfarer. I do not say, "Remember me now," but, "when You come in Your kingdom."

---

[26] Cf. Tertulian, *Against the Marcionites*, 3.23; *Against the Jews*, 13 ("The clouds being celestial benefits which were commanded not to be forthcoming to the house of Israel; for it *'had borne thorns,'* whereof that house of Israel had wrought a crown for Christ."); *Constitution of the Apostles*, 6.5 ("He has taken away from them the Holy Spirit and the prophetic rain, and has replenished His Church with spiritual grace.").

Take the Example of the Thief on the Right

What power, O robber, led you to the light? Who taught you to worship that despised Man, your companion on the Cross? O Light Eternal, Who gives light to those who are in darkness! Therefore also he justly heard the words, "Be of good cheer"[27]—not that your deeds are worthy of good cheer; but that the King is here, dispensing favors.

The request reached unto a distant time; but the grace was very speedy: "'Truly, Truly I say unto you, today you will be with Me in Paradise' (Luke 23:43); because 'Today if you hear [My] voice, do not harden your hearts' (Psalms 94:7, 8). Very speedily I passed sentence upon Adam, very speedily I pardon you. To him it was said, 'In the day in which you eat of it, you shall surely die' (Genesis 2:17); but you today have obeyed the faith, today is your salvation. Adam fell away by the Tree; you by the Tree are brought into Paradise. Fear not the serpent; he shall not cast you out; for he is fallen from heaven (Luke 10:18). And I will say not unto you, 'This day you will depart,' but, 'This day you will be with Me. Be of good courage: you will not be cast out. Fear not the flaming sword (cf. Genesis 3:24); it shrinks from its Lord ."[28]

O mighty and ineffable grace! The faithful Abraham had not yet entered, but the robber enters![29] Moses and the prophets had not yet entered, and the robber enters though a breaker of the law. Paul also wondered at this before you, saying, "Where sin abounded, grace abound much more" (Romans 5:20). Those who had borne the heat of the day had not yet entered; and he of the

---

[27] An introduction to Luke 23:43 in *Codex Bezae*.

[28] "All who desire to return to Paradise must be tried by fire: for not in vain the Scripture says that when Adam and Eve were driven out of their abode in Paradise, God placed at the gate of Eden a flaming sword which turned every way." St. Ambrose, *Sermon* 20.12 on Psalm 119.

[29] Cf. St. Irenaeus 5.5.1; St. Athanasius, *Expositio Fidei*, 1: "He showed us... an entrance into Paradise from which Adam was cast out, and into which he entered again by means of the thief."

eleventh hour entered. Let none murmur against the owner of the house, for he says, "Friend, I do you no wrong; is it not lawful for Me to do what I will with My own?" (Matthew 20:12 ff.)

The robber has a will to work righteousness, but death prevents him; I wait not exclusively for the work, but faith also I accept. "I have come Who feed My sheep among the lilies" (Song of Songs 6:3). I have come to feed them in the gardens. I have found a sheep that was lost (Luke 15:5, 6); but I lay it on My shoulders. For he believes, since he himself has said, "I have gone astray like a lost sheep" (Psalms 118:176). "Lord, remember me when You come in Your kingdom."

The Altar of His Body

Of this garden I sang of old to My spouse in the Canticles, and spoke to her saying: "I am come into My garden, My sister, My spouse" (Song of Songs 6:1). Now in the place where He was crucified was a garden (John 19:41), what brings You there? "I have gathered My myrrh; having drunk wine mingled with myrrh, and vinegar," after receiving which, He said, "It is finished" (John 19:30).

For the mystery has been fulfilled; the things that are written have been accomplished; sins are forgiven. Christ having come as High Priest of the good things to come, by the greater and more perfect tabernacle, not made with hands, that is to say, not of this creation, nor yet by the blood of goats and calves, but by His own blood, entered in once for all into the holy place, having obtained eternal redemption; for if the blood of bulls and of goats, and the ashes of an heifer, sprinkling the defiled, sanctifies the purifying of the flesh, how much more the blood of Christ?" (Hebrews 9:11-14).

And again, "Having therefore, brethren, boldness to enter into the holiest by the blood of Jesus, by a new and living way, which He has consecrated for us, through the veil, that is to say, His flesh" (Hebrews 10:19, 20). And because His flesh, this veil, was dishonored, therefore the typical veil of the temple was rent asunder, as it is written, "And, behold, the veil of the temple was torn in two from the top to the bottom" (Matthew 27:51). For not a particle of it was left; for since the Master said, "Behold, your house is left unto you desolate" (Matthew 23:38), the house is all destroyed in pieces.

His Righteousness is Greater than Our Sins.

These things the Savior endured, and "made peace through the Blood of His Cross, for things in heaven, and things in earth" (Colossians 1:20, 21). For we were enemies of God through sin, and God had appointed the sinner to die. Therefore, one of two things must have happened: either that God, in His truth, should destroy all men, or that in His loving-kindness He should cancel the sentence.

But, behold the wisdom of God. He preserved both the truth of His sentence, and the exercise of His loving-kindness. Christ "bore our sins in His own body on the tree, that we by His death might die to sin, and live for righteousness" (1 Peter 2:24).

Of no small account was He who died for us; He was not a literal sheep; He was not a mere man; He was more than an angel; He was God made man. The transgression of sinners was not so great as the righteousness of Him who died for them; the sin which we committed was not so great as the righteousness which He wrought who laid down His life for us,–Who laid it down when He pleased, and took it again when He pleased. And would you know that He laid not down His life by violence, nor yielded up the spirit against His will? He cried to the Father, saying, Father, "Into Your hands I commend My Spirit" (Luke 23:46). I commend it, that I may take it again. "And having said these things, He yielded up His spirit" (Matthew 27:50). But not for any long time, for He quickly rose again from the dead.

He is the Sun of Righteousness and the Spiritual Rock

The sun was darkened because of the "Sun of Righteousness" (Malachi 4:2). The rocks were split because of the spiritual Rock (1 Corinthians 10:4). The tombs were opened, and the dead arose, because of Him Who was "free among the dead" (Psalms 87:5); for He freed His "prisoners out of the pit having no water" (Zechariah 9:11).

So then, do not be ashamed of the Crucified, but be you also bold to say, "He bears our sins for us, and endures grief for us...and by His stripes we are healed" (Isaiah 53:4, 5). Let us not be unthankful to our Benefactor. And again, "for the transgression of My people was He led to death; and I will give the wicked for His burial, and the rich for His death" (Isaiah 53: 8, 9). Therefore Paul says plainly, "that Christ died for our sins according to the Scriptures, and that He was buried, and that He has risen again the third day according to the Scriptures" (1 Corinthians 15:3, 4).

The Prophesies Concerning His Tomb and the Door

But we seek to know clearly where He has been buried. Is His tomb made with hands? Is it, like the tombs of kings, raised above the ground? Is the Sepulcher made of stones joined together? And what is laid upon it? Tell us, O Prophets, the exact truth concerning His tomb also, where He is laid, and where we shall seek Him?

And they say, "Look into the solid rock which you have hewn" (Isaiah 51:1). Look in and behold. You also have written in the gospels, the same: In a sepulcher hewn in stone, which was hewn out of a rock (Matthew 27:60; Mark 15:46; Luke 23:50).

And what happens next? What kind of door has the sepulcher? Again another Prophet says, "They cut off My life in a dungeon" (Lamentations 3:53; cf. Jeremiah 37:16); and cast a stone upon Me, I, who am "the Chief corner-stone, the elect, the precious" (1 Peter 2:6), lie for a little time within a stone–I who am a stone of stumbling to the Jews, and of salvation to them who believe. Therefore, the Tree of life (Genesis 2:9; 3:22) was planted

in the earth, that the earth which had been cursed might enjoy the blessing, and that the dead might be released.[30]

The Power of the Sign of the Cross

Let us not then be ashamed to confess the Crucified. Let the Cross be our seal made with boldness by our fingers on our brow, and on everything; over the bread we eat, and the cups we drink; in our comings in, and goings out; before our sleep, when we lie down and when we rise up; when we are in the way, and when we are still.[31]

Great is that preservative; it is without price, for the sake of the poor; without toil, for the sick; since also its grace is from God. It is the Sign of the faithful, and the dread of devils: for He triumphed over them in it, "having made a public spectacle out of them" (Colossians 2:15). For when they see the Cross they are reminded of the Crucified; they are afraid of Him, who "bruised the heads of the dragons" (Psalms 73:13). Despise not the Seal, because of the freeness of the gift, but rather honor your Benefactor for this.

The Cross and Salvation

And if you ever fall into disputation and have not the grounds of proof, yet let faith remain firm in you; or rather, become you well learned, and then silence the Jews out of the prophets, and the Greeks out of their own fables. They themselves worship men who have been thunder-stricken but the thunder when it comes from heaven, it does not come randomly. If they are not ashamed to worship men thunder-stricken and abhorred of God, are you ashamed to worship the beloved Son of God, who was crucified for you?

---

[30] "He who has not believed in Christ, nor has understood that He is the first principle and the Tree of Life, etc..." (Methodius, *Sympos.* 9.3)

[31] Cf. St. Cyril of Jerusalem, *Catechetical Homilies*, 4.14; Eusebius, *Dem. Ev.*, 9.14.

I am ashamed to tell the tales about their so-called gods, and I leave them because of time; let those who know, speak. And let all heretics also be silenced. If anyone says that the Cross is an illusion, turn away from him. Abhor those who say that Christ was crucified to our fancy only; for if so, and if salvation is from the Cross, then is salvation a fancy also. If the Cross is fancy, the Resurrection is fancy also; but "if Christ is not risen, we are still in our sins" (1 Corinthians 15:17). If the Cross is fancy, the Ascension also is fancy; and if the Ascension is fancy, then is the second coming also fancy, and everything is henceforth unsubstantial.

You Are Accusers if You Deny the Cross

Take therefore first, as an indestructible foundation, the Cross, and build upon it the other articles of the faith. Do not deny the Crucified; for, if you deny Him, you have many to arraign you. Judas the traitor will arraign you first; for he who betrayed Him knows that He was condemned to death by the chief-priests and elders.

The thirty pieces of silver bear witness; Gethsemane bears witness, where the betrayal occurred; I have not spoken yet of the Mount of Olives, on which they were with Him at night, praying. The moon in the night bears witness; the day bears witness, and the sun which was darkened; for it endured not to look on the crime of the conspirators. The fire will arraign you, by which Peter stood and warmed himself; if you deny the Cross, the eternal fire awaits you. I speak hard words, that you may not experience hard pains. Remember the swords that came against Him in Gethsemane, that you feel not the eternal sword.

The house of Caiaphas,[32] will arraign you, showing by its present desolation the power of Him who was some time ago judged there. Yes, Caiaphas himself will rise up against you in the day of judgment, the very servant will rise up against you, who smote Jesus with the palm of his hand; they also who bound Him, and they who led Him away. Even Herod shall rise up against you; and Pilate; as if saying, "Why do you deny Him Who was slandered before us by the Jews, and whom we knew to have done no wrong? For I Pilate then washed my hands."

The false witnesses shall rise up against you, and the soldiers who arrayed Him in the purple robe, and set on Him the crown of thorns, and crucified Him in Golgotha, and cast lots for His coat. Simon the Cyrenian will cry out upon you, who bore the Cross after Jesus.

From among the stars there will cry out upon you, the darkened Sun; among the things upon earth, the Wine mingled with myrrh; among reeds, the Reed; among herbs, the Hyssop; among the things of the sea, the Sponge; among trees, the Wood of the Cross;–the soldiers, too, as I have said, who nailed Him, and cast lots for His garments; the soldier who pierced His side with the spear; the women who then were present; the veil of the temple then rent asunder; the hall of Pilate, now laid waste by the power of Him who was then crucified; this holy Golgotha, which stands high above us, and shows itself to this day, and displays even

---

[32] The house of Caiaphas and Pilate's Praetorium (§41), and Mount Zion itself (Cat. 16.18), on which they both stood are described as ruined and desolate (cf. Eusebius, *Dem. Ev.*, 8.406). Micah's prophesy in 3:12, repeated by Jeremiah in 26:18, mention that Zion shall be plowed as a field, and Jerusalem shall become heaps, testifies that he had seen with his own eyes the place being plowed and sown by strangers, and adds that in his own time the stones for both public and private buildings were taken from the ruins. Also, The Bordeaux Pilgrim (333 A.D.) says, "It is evident where the house of Caiaphas the Priest was; and there is still the pillar at which Christ was scourged." This pillar is described by St. Jerome (*Epistle* 86) as supporting the portico of the Church which by his time had been built on the spot (cf. Prudentius c. 400 AD).

yet how because of Christ the rocks were then split; the sepulcher nigh at hand where He was laid; and the stone which was laid on the door, which lies to this day by the tomb; the angels who were then present; the women who worshipped Him after His resurrection; Peter and John, who ran to the sepulcher; and Thomas, who thrust his hand into His side, and his fingers into the prints of the nails. For it was for our sakes that he so carefully handled Him; and what you, who were not there present, would have sought, he being present, by God's Providence, did seek.

The Trophy of Salvation

You have Twelve Apostles, witnesses of the Cross; and the whole earth, and the world of men who believe on Him Who hung thereon. Let your very presence here now persuade you of the power of the Crucified. For who now brought you to this assembly? What soldiers? With what bonds were you constrained? What sentence held you fast here now?

No, it was the Trophy of salvation, the Cross of Jesus that brought you all together. It was this that enslaved the Persians, and tamed the Scythians; this that gave to the Egyptians, for cats and dogs and their manifold errors, the knowledge of God; this, that to this day heals diseases; that to this day drives away devils, and overthrows the tricks of drugs and charms.

Δοξὰ ϲι ὁ Θεοϲ ἡμων

APPENDIX OF CHURCH FATHERS

St. Ambrose of Milan (340-397 A.D.)

He was born in Trier, Arles or Lyons, from a Roman, Christian family. His father, Ambrosius was a prefect of Gallia Narbonensis (which included France, Britain and Spain), and had a sister Marcellina (who became a nun), and a brother Satyrus, who also became a prefect. With his classical and legal education he was assigned to a government post around Milan around 370. In 373-374 he was baptized and ordained as bishop by popular demand after a child cried out, "Bishop Ambrose," and the crowd responded, apparently against Ambrose's will. St. Ambrose highly influenced St. Augustine, guided him back to the true faith, and baptized him. His major work on the New Testament was a commentary on the Gospel of Luke. He also wrote treatises such as To the New Emperor Gratian, and On the Holy Spirit (381), which is taken largely from St. Basil the Great's treatise on the same subject. He mastered the Greek language and literature. Upon his death Paulinus write his biography.

St. Athanasius the Apostolic (c. 295-373 A.D.)

This great St. is called the Apostolic by the Coptic Orthodox Church because he is considered a successor to the apostles due to his erudite theological and biblical teaching. We know little about his childhood, except for an incident in which he was baptizing children by the sea, and was discovered by Pope Alexander, who later began to teach the young Athanasius. He spent three years in the desert under the guidance of St. Antony the Great, along with St. Serapion. He spent six years as a reader in Alexandria, was later ordained as a deacon by Pope Alexander, and helped at the Council of Nicaea in 325. According to the Coptic Encomium, he was 33 when he was ordained as pope and patriarch in 328. He fought diligently against Arius and his teachings. He was exiled five times and spent 16 of his 46 years as pope in exile. Among his writings are On the Incarnation, Three Orations against the Arians, The Life of Antony, Against Appolinarius, and various epistles to monks and bishops.

St. Augustine (354-430 A.D.)

He was a prolific father of the church born in Tagasta, North Africa to Patritius, his pagan father and Roman official, and Monica, his faithful Christian mother. At the age of 16, he went to Carthage to study law, literature, and philosophy. He became a teacher of rhetoric in Tagaste, Carthage, and Rome, taught in Rome and Milan, and lived a sinful life. His famous prayer in resisting God, was "Give me chastity and continence, but not yet." Due to the prayers of his mother, the intellect and competence of St. Ambrose of Milan, St. Athanasius' amazing biography of St. Antony, and the impact of Romans 13:13, he was finally baptized at the age of 33 (in 387). In the same year, St. Monica departed. He returned to Italy, established a monastery there, was ordained a priest, and later a bishop of Hippo. He would have attended the Council of Nicaea, but he departed when Barbarians were attacking his diocese in Hippo. His extant writings include the Confessions, the City of God, Commentaries on the Old and New Testaments, On the Trinity, On Rebuke and Grace, Against the Manicheeans, and The perseverance of the St.s, which is his last major work. Despite many of his wonderful writings, prayers, and contemplations, he is also attributed with being the source of many incorrect teachings such as the filioque, the doctrine of original sin and grace, predestination, purgatory, and other such beliefs. Many claim this was due to his lack of Greek, and thus his lack of knowledge of the Eastern fathers.

St. Cyril of Alexandria (c. 380-444 A.D.)

Also known as the Pillar of Faith, this father is the twenty-fourth Patriarch of the See of St. Mark. St. Cyril was the son of the sister of Pope Theophilus (23rd patriarch), who trained him in Theology and Philosophy at the School of Alexandria, then sent

THE FEAST OF THE CROSS

him to the monastery of St. Macarius in the wilderness. There he studied the Church books and sayings of the fathers for five years under a righteous monk named Sarapamon. Later he was sent to the honorable bishop Abba Serapion, and he increased in wisdom and knowledge. After St. Cyril returned to Alexandria, Pope Theophilus ordained him a deacon, appointed him a preacher in the cathedral, and made St. Cyril his scribe. When his uncle departed in 412, St. Cyril was enthroned as patriarch on 20 Babeh, 128 AM (October 17, 412). He is famous for his exceptional biblical exegesis and Christological formulas, which he used to defend the faith while presiding over the Council of Ephesus against Nestorius. He remained a pope for 31 years. He is one of the greatest fathers of the ancient Church, whose life and teachings have been decisive in shaping the Orthodox tradition.

St. Cyril of Jerusalem

Not much is known about his early life, but he was ordained a priest at Jerusalem before 343. Around 348, he was appointed bishop of Jerusalem, despite the attacks from leaders of other sects, and being exiled three separate times. He is most famous for his Catechetical Lectures, which were written for those desiring to join the Christian faith (although a few scholars have attributed this to his successor, John of Jerusalem). His messages focused on the importance of the death and Resurrection of our Lord Jesus Christ.

St. Ephrem the Syrian (c. 306-373 A.D.)

One of the early fathers of the church from Syria. He was among those who attended the Council of Nicaea. He is famous for his poetical hymns, especially those relating to the Annunciation, Nativity, and Holy Theotokos. He wrote a famous commentary on Tatian's Diatessaron, the Book of Daniel, and the Pauline Epistles. Often he quoted the Peshitta translation, which is among the earliest manuscripts of the Old Testament today. His writings well represent the Syrian patristic tradition. He is also known for his famous visit to St. Pishoy in Egypt, in what is now El-Surian (The Syrian) Monastery.

St. Gregory of Nazianzus "the Theologian" (c. 330-389 A.D.)

This father was born at the country estate belonging to his father called Arianzus, near Nazianzus–a place quite unknown to early writers. His parents were rich Christian landowners and his father was bishop of Nazianzus. Gregory studied in the major centers of learning before being baptized in 358. His father forced him to accept ordination as a priest in 361. In 371, his friend Basil unsuccessfully attempted to persuade him to accept being ordained as a bishop. However, eight years later, St. Gregory finally agreed to accept the responsibility of being the bishop of Constantinople in 379, where he served for two years before resigning. His poetry and theological writings earned him the title of the Theologian. He is considered to be among the Cappadocian Fathers, which include St. Basil and St. Gregory of Nyssa.

St. Gregory the Wonder-Worker ("Thaumaturgos") (210-260 A.D.)

He was the enthusiastic disciple of Origen, and the apostle of Pontus. He was born at Neo-Caesarea in Pontus, and destined for some kind of civil career, but happened to come to Caesarea in Palestine, where Origen had settled down shortly before (in 231). He remained there, studying under his tutorship, for eight years. Before he returned home, he wrote his panegyrics on his great teacher, and shortly after his arrival home he was consecrated bishop of his native city by Phaedimus of Amisus. He found seventeen Christians in Neo-Caesarea when he entered his office: there were only seventeen pagans left when he died (about 270). Testimonies of the energy he developed and the influence he exercised are not only the legends which cluster around his name, but also the writings he left–his so-called canonical letter on discipline–one of the most interesting documents of ancient

Christianity, the confession he used for the catechumens of his church, and his paraphrase of Ecclesiastes.

St. Ignatius of Antioch (d. 107 A.D.)

One of the most famous disciples of St. John the Beloved, St. Ignatius was consecrated bishop over the city of Antioch. He is famous for his seven pastoral letters–the Ephesians, Magnesians, Romans, Philadelphians, Smyrna, Tralles, and Polycarp–that were written between 100-107 AD. Although he does not quote from the Old testament, he had a strong focus on eschatology as well as church unity. The theology of his writings foreshadows the later definitions of the Ecumenical Councils.

St. Jerome (350-420 A.D.)

He was born as Sophronius Eusebius Hieronymous and soon showed immense potential as a scholar. He lived for a while in Jerusalem, then was summoned by Pope Damasus of Rome in 382 to revise the Latin translation of the Bible, called the Vulgate. He completed his revision of the Gospels in 383/4, but seems to have largely abandoned the work to devote his energies to the Hebrew Old Testament. He died in 419/20. Besides his translations (which include patristic works as well as the Vulgate), he left a number of letters and assorted commentaries plus biographies of "Famous Men." Interestingly, the text used by Jerome in his commentaries often differs from that in the Vulgate.

St. John Chrysostom (347-407 A.D.)

St. John Chrysostom was born in Antioch between 347 and 349. His father was a soldier in Syria and his mother was a faithful Christian. After his father died when he was very young, he was raised by his mother, Anthusa. He was so gifted that she arranged for him to study Philosophy, Rhetoric, and Greek. He agreed with two of his classmates, Evagrius and Basil (most probably not Basil the Great), to seek the monastic life, but because of the tears of his mother he agreed to continue his education as an advocate (lawyer) instead. At the age of 18, he studied under Patriarch Meletius, who encouraged him to stay with him. At 21, he was baptized, and three years later, he was ordained a reader and composed Against the Jews and many pamphlets. After deceiving his friend, Basil, into ordination, John defended himself with the treatise On the Priesthood. Upon the death of his mother, he gave all his goods to the poor, chose one of the poorest monasteries, and meditated on the Scriptures and wrote three treatises on the monastic life. He was later ordained as a deacon, and wrote many more treatises. The Patriarch Flavian ordained him as priest. Some called him "the mouth of Christ," others "a second Paul," and others the "golden-mouthed (Chrysostom)." This last name was given to him by a woman during one of his sermons. He was ordained the bishop of Constantinople by force in 398. His sermons led the city through many crises, but his enemies eventually exiled him three times. He spent his last days of his earthly life in exile.

St. Justin the Martyr (b. 100-110; d. 163-167 A.D.)

He was born into a pagan family in Samaria between 100 and 110 AD. After practicing Stoic, Peripatetic, and Pythagorean philosophies, he finally converted to Christianity most probably in Ephesus. Due to his philosophical background, he is the first Christian thinker to seek to reconcile the claims of faith and reason. Among his many works, he is most famous for his Apology (c. 155 AD), addressed to Emperor Antoninus Pius and his colleagues; as well as his Dialogue with Trypho, a discussion with a Jew named Trypho about the differences in the two faiths. These, among his other works, make him one of the most important of the apologists of the second century and one of the noblest personalities of early Christian literature. Clothed in the palladium, a cloak worn by Greek philosophers, he traveled about, an itinerant teacher. He arrived in Rome during the reign of Antoninus Pius (138-161 A.D) and founded a school there. One of his pupils was Tatian, destined later to become an apologist. St. Justin suffered martyrdom in Rome between 163 and 167 AD.

Methodius of Olympus (c. 311 A.D.)

He was a polished writer and an opponent of Origenism–his name is consequently passed over without mention by the Origenist historian Eusebius. We have his Banquet in Greek, and some smaller works in Old Slavonic. He also accepted the idea of an earthly millennium in which justice and peace reign on earth at the end times (Revelation 19).

The Scholar Origen (185-254 A.D.)

He was born into a Christian family: his father Leonides was a righteous scholar who was martyred during the persecution of Septimius Severus in 202 AD. At an early age, Origen dedicated his life to reading and scholarly endeavors. St. Jerome praised his love of reading and said that Origen read while eating, walking, resting, etc. When Pope Demetrius, the twelfth Patriarch of Alexandria, heard of his fame, he appointed him dean of the School of Alexandria. He increased its fame and thinking and became a teacher of many bishops and priests, as well as many men, women, young and old. He was famous for his allegorical interpretation, such as his famous interpretation of the Song of Songs. He was imprisoned and tortured for his Christian faith. He was courageous, ascetic and a man of fasting and prayer. He exaggerated in his asceticism by castrating himself (defending his action by saying that he was protecting his chastity). He was such a prolific writer that some of his admirers said, "There is no human mind that can absorb all what he wrote." St. Epiphanius (315-403 AD) stated that Origen had 6,000 manuscripts, including his famous Hexapla, 28-year study comparing six manuscripts of the Old Testament and their translations. Pope Demetrius excommunicated Origen for theological mistakes, as well as being ordained in Palestine, outside of his diocese. He spent the rest of his time there, where he established a famous theological school.

He is one of the most controversial as well as influential ancient writers.

St. Polycarp of Smyrna (d. 155-156 A.D.)

He was another famous disciple of St. John the Apostle, who is well known in the writings of St. Ignatius of Antioch, who wrote him a personal letter before his own martyrdom. As Bishop of Smyrna, he devoted much energy to preserve the pure Christian faith against the heresies of the Marcionites and the Valentinians. Eventually he was martyred at the age of 86, in 155 or 156 AD. We have detailed accounts of St. Polycarp's martyrdom, from the community surrounding Philomelium.

Socrates Scholasticus (b. 380 A.D.)

He was also called Socrates of Constantinople writes and quotes from the historian Eusebius, while completing much of his work with additional information of the Church history from the conversion of Constantine to about 439 AD. He begins by narrating "The particulars which he has left out" through various documents and other sources. His writings are found in NPNF, s. 2, v. 2.

Sozomen the Historian or Salminius Hermias Sozomenus (c. 400-450 A.D.)

He was a Church historian from Palestine. The church history he composed focuses on the era between 323 and 425 AD in 9 books. One of his main focuses in the work is to present how the Jews were very stubborn in not accepting God the Word. His writings are also included in NPNF, s. 2, v. 2, following that of Socrates Scholasticus.

The Scholar Tertullian (c.160-225 A.D.)

He was a scholar born to a pagan family in Carthage, North Africa. His father was a Roman centurion. He received a good education in Literature and Rhetoric, practiced law in Rome, and visited Athens and Rome in his youth. He was converted to Christianity before 197 AD and returned to his native city as a Christian shortly before the turn of the third century. He wrote extensively against the various enemies of the church. But, like many converts, the fixed life of the official church was not sufficient for him. He wanted a return to prophecy. After some years of trying and failing to restore the spiritual nature of the Church in the West, he became a Montanist (c. 207). St. Jerome reported that this happened in his "middle age." According to St. Jerome, he became a priest, but there are other indications that he remained a layman. Shortly after 220, Tertullian seems to have tried to form an independent congregation before his death. He was the author of a long list of apologetic, theological, and ascetic works. No list of Tertullian's works is extant, but historians have identified at least 43 titles, of which all or part 31 survive. Some of these, however, were written after he left the Church. Among his Apologetic writings he addressed a work To the Heathen (Ad Nations, two books), in which he protested against the laws condemning Christians without examining their behavior. Nevertheless, St. Cyprian called him "the master," and made it a policy to read from his works every day. Tertullian's text is rather unique, as he wrote in Latin but apparently used primarily Greek texts which he translated himself. One historian says, "He touched almost nothing which he did not exaggerate."